DRAWING FOR ARCHITECTURE

Writing **Architecture** series

A project of the Anyone Corporation

Earth Moves: The Furnishing of Territories
Bernard Cache, 1995

Architecture as Metaphor: Language, Number, Money
Kojin Karatani, 1995

Differences: Topographies of Contemporary Architecture
Ignasi de Solà-Morales, 1996

Constructions
John Rajchman, 1997

Such Places as Memory
John Hejduk, 1998

Welcome to the Hotel Architecture
Roger Connah, 1998

Fire and Memory: On Architecture and Energy
Luis Fernández-Galiano, 2000

A Landscape of Events
Paul Virilio, 2000

Architecture from the Outside: Essays on Virtual and Real Space
Elizabeth Grosz, 2001

Public Intimacy: Architecture and the Visual Arts
Giuliana Bruno, 2007

Strange Details
Michael Cadwell, 2007

Histories of the Immediate Present: Inventing Architectural Modernism
Anthony Vidler, 2008

Drawing for Architecture
Léon Krier, 2009

DRAWING FOR ARCHITECTURE

LÉON KRIER

FOREWORD BY JAMES HOWARD KUNSTLER

THE MIT PRESS

CAMBRIDGE, MASSACHUSETTS

LONDON, ENGLAND

MIT Press books may be purchased at special quantity discounts for business or sales promotional use.
For information, please email special_sales@mitpress.mit.edu or write to Special Sales Department, The MIT Press, 55 Hayward Street, Cambridge, MA 02142.

This book was set in Filosofia by Graphic Composition, Inc.
Printed and bound in Spain.

Library of Congress Cataloging-in-Publication Data

Krier, Léon.
Drawing for architecture / Léon Krier ; foreword by James Howard Kunstler.
p. cm.— (Writing architecture)
ISBN 978-0-262-51293-0 (pbk. : alk. paper)
1. Architecture, Modern—20th century—Pictorial works. 2. City planning—History—20th century—Pictorial works. 3. Krier, Léon—Notebooks, sketchbooks, etc. I. Title.
NA680.K683 2009
720.22′2—dc22

2008039055

10 9 8 7 6 5 4 3 2 1

CONTENTS

FOREWORD

In 2005, Léon Krier and I discovered we were on the same page, so to speak, where the larger questions of how we live were beginning to press in on us. By *how we live* I mean not only what mankind's physical dwelling place will be as the twenty-first century staggers on, but whether civilized existence per se might continue—and by *civilized* I mean very precisely the operation of our towns and cities.

Around that time, an awareness was rising in the West that the very basis for modern culture would soon be threatened by a permanent global energy crisis. The shorthand for this crisis was the term *Peak Oil*, which proposed a number of explicit conditions and implied many more. Explicitly, it said that the fossil-fueled industrial age was likely to wind down from sheer resource exhaustion (and the news from the so-called alternative energy scene was not reassuring that anything else would offset those losses). Beyond this, Peak Oil implied that the many complex systems we rely on for modern life would founder sooner rather than later, once the world oil production peak was achieved and we started down the nauseating slope of depletion—a situation that now appears to be the case. *Complex systems* are anything from the way we produce our food, to the way we conduct commerce, to the way we inhabit the terrain, to the way we move about the terrain. Finance, the deployment and management of capital, is a particularly sensitive complex system that is cracking up globally even as I write. This is, in no small part, because Peak Oil portends the end of regularized cyclical industrial growth and its valid representation in paper certificates, which are the stock-in-trade of finance.

The Peak Oil situation was significant for Krier because it presented compelling new support for his campaign to restore traditional practices in architecture and urbanism—namely, that continuation of the broad modern(ist) program would soon be a practical impossibility. The generalized urban hypertrophy that characterized the twentieth century had been underwritten by oil and methane (natural) gas. Everything from the skyscraper to the American happy motoring suburb stood to lose value and utility in the aftermath of an oil supply crash. The fabricated, resource-and-energy-intensive materials that so delighted the architectural modernists—the metal panels, beams, trusses, high-tech veneers, reinforced concretes, and plastic epoxies—would become increasingly scarce. Materials found in nature regionally would return by necessity, along with methods of assembly that could only be expressed tectonically as some sort of classicism. The increment of new development would necessarily revert to a scale more agreeable with human neurology and physiology. The scale of the urban organism would have to revert downward. Peak Oil provided real urgency for Krier's ideas. The ideology of his modernist opponents, whether framed as metaphysics or high fashion, withered in the face of these reality-based arguments.

In any case, Krier's positions, dating back to his early career in the 1970s, remained no less valid when joined by the new resource imperatives. He had inveighed against the excesses of modernism for twenty-five years in fluent, muscular polemics, while presenting a fresh, graceful, and comprehensive counter-vision to the disciples of Le Corbusier and Mies van der Rohe. He was particularly thorough and eloquent on the discipline of typology—the lexicon of categories that the modernists had consigned to history's garbage barge—and without which the syntaxes of architecture and urbanism had descended into a sordid glossolalia.

Krier's polemical books were always accompanied by drawings, diagrams, and cartoons, which illustrated his points with tremendous economy and wit. This was a good tactic for a crusader attempting to penetrate the mental defenses of opponents who hid behind the sandbags of ideology and "artistic creativity." In these drawings, the verbally adept could be engaged by direct appeal to the brain's higher cognitive courts, where their metaphysical torts would be dismissed by more persuasive graphic evidence; the artistic creatives could be hoisted easily on the petards of their own pretension by straightforward depictions of the self-evident. Krier's drawings were especially effective combating the confusion sown by the modernists' deliberate obscurantism. The potency of his drawings derives from our recognition that a persistent reality still exists, and that it endures despite the intellectual legerdemain of those who say they create their own reality.

Krier's drawings often take the form of a *dialectic*, a presentation of the relations between two opposing ideas: industry versus craft, classical versus vernacular, modernist versus traditional, and so on. Other cases are presented as lessons using the shorthand of pictures in a manner that has greater impact than a mere recitation of the facts—for instance, his pictorial discussion of the defects in the standard Berlin city block and its remedy, a complicated affair that Krier very effectively limits to a one-page graphic.

These oppositions and contradictions are as self-consciously polemical in his drawings as in his writings. Krier always presents an argument and takes a clear position. These positions derive from a coherent and comprehensive worldview, one that apprehends the extraordinary diminishing returns of the techno-triumphalism that defined the twentieth century, its intellectual movements, plus its aesthetic obsessions and the ensuing destruction of our human dwelling places that resulted from these things. Krier's work amounts to a catalog of clarified and rectified principles—fundamental truths that have been confused, abused, and misused so consistently by the mandarins of academic architecture and the officialdom of urban planning that it has become all but impossible in our time to create buildings and places worthy of our affection. Of course, the product of all this confusion and abuse is visible on the ground all over the United States, and increasingly in other nations, in the strip malls, parking wastelands, skyscrapers, landscrapers, "housing" monocultures, and other dismal effluvia of the age now ending.

Léon Krier's work has been a superb corrective to all this, though his campaign has sometimes been a lonely one, and the sheer inertia built into the modernist zeitgeist has fortified it mightily against any attempt at reform. In this new book, his drawings stand on their own without the assistance of his usually sturdy prose. In their superb clarity and simplicity they resist misinterpretation. They champion the actual over the abstract, the truthful over the mendacious, the organic over the artificial, and the graceful over the soulless. Krier presents some of his ideas in several sequential versions, each one self-sufficiently ingenious.

Because they are pictures, they might make an impression on a younger generation more attuned to imagery than to rhetoric. The world these young practitioners inherit will be very different from the fiesta of comfort and convenience that has been the norm in Western industrial life since the end of the Second World War. I think Léon Krier and I are both serenely confident that we are in for big changes. I anticipate that these new circumstances will compel us to make other arrangements for virtually all the activities of everyday life. They will change everything about how we inhabit the landscape, and they will certainly require us to reconnect with the forsaken traditional principles of architecture and urbanism. Léon Krier's new book of drawings will become one of the seminal volumes of a future that is almost here.

James Howard Kunstler
Saratoga Springs, New York

L. K.
2002

AUTHOR'S NOTE

In addition to my architectural and urban projects, I produce a great number of doodles, ideograms that are the subject of this volume. They are not a natural occupation; they only come to me in discontinuous, short, and generally angry bursts. They often sum up in one or two images what I had been previously trying to articulate in projects, writings, or speech. The first of such outbreaks came in 1980 after a protracted writing sweat, when in a few days I summarized two hundred pages of text in approximately the same number of ideograms. These have mostly a stringent undertone; they are, in fact, counterattacks against endured aggressions, absurdities, and paradoxes, with which life is so richly endowed.

Raw and without circumlocution, these ideograms are means not to console or please but to reveal scandalous elements of architectural practices and ideology; they outline conceptual tools for refounding traditional urbanism and architecture. It is well known that actions cause reactions mostly of an unexpected or unintended kind. What will win as the end of human activities, of fulfilled or frustrated lives? The good or the bad, the right or the wrong, the intelligent or the stupid? Evidently neither human nor artificial intelligence gains notable insight into ultimate issues. We can, however, no longer ignore that in matters of settlement, building, and energy policies, industrial civilization is engaged in a tragic impasse. We now generally build in the wrong places, in the wrong patterns, materials, types, densities, and heights, and for the wrong number of dwellers.

In my opinion, the traditional architecture and building and settlement techniques of the pre–fossil fuel age represent the operative tools of global ecological reconstruction. It is the condition of nature that will, as in the past, redefine our development possibilities. These doodles may help to point our thinking in that direction.

Léon Krier

CONSTRUCTION

vernacular Building

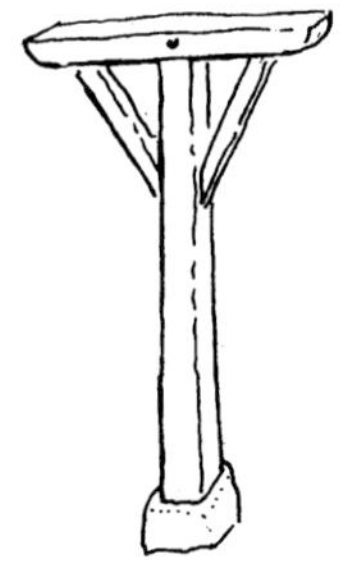

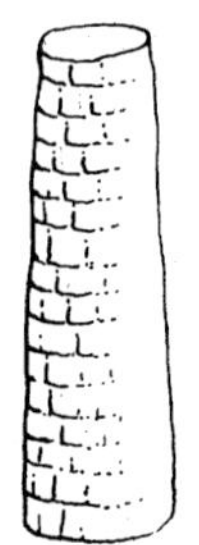

CLASSICAL ARCHITECTURE

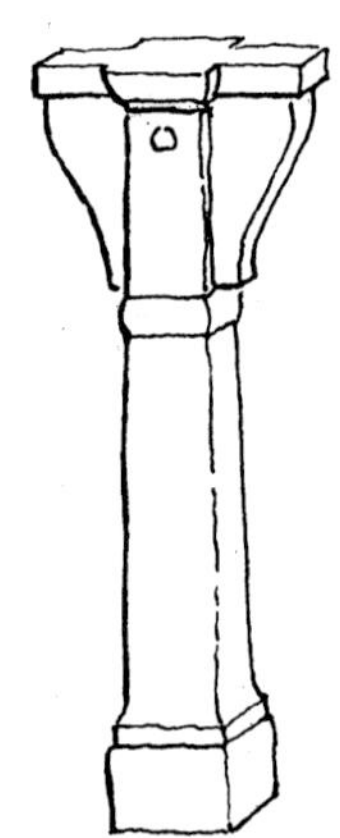

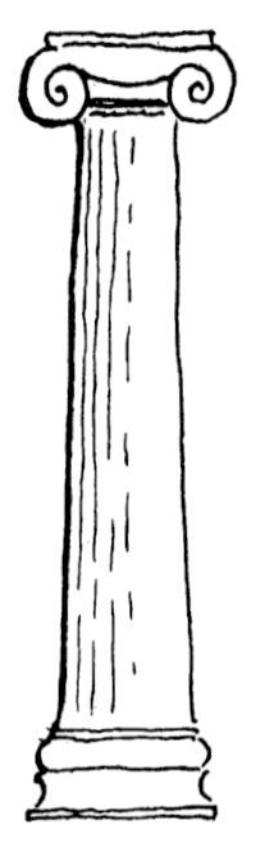

SIZE × TYPE × EXPRESSION

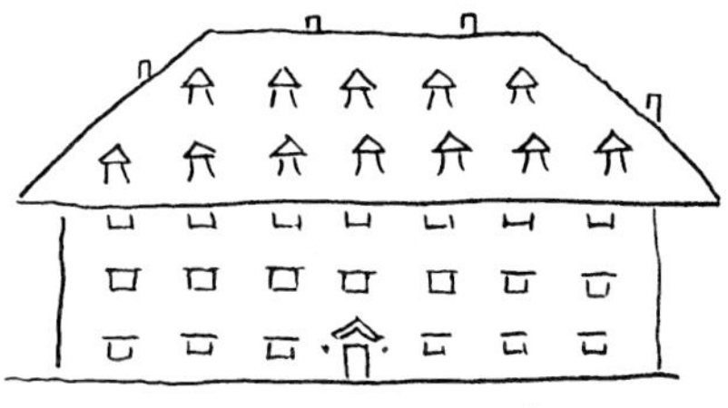

Cottage PALACE~SIZE
"COTTAGE LOOK"

PALACE Cottage-size
"PALACE LOOK"

VERNACULAR X classical

USE & MISUSE

PALACE ~ PALACE-SIZE

Cottage ~ Cottage size

CLASSICAL & vernacular

LK 03

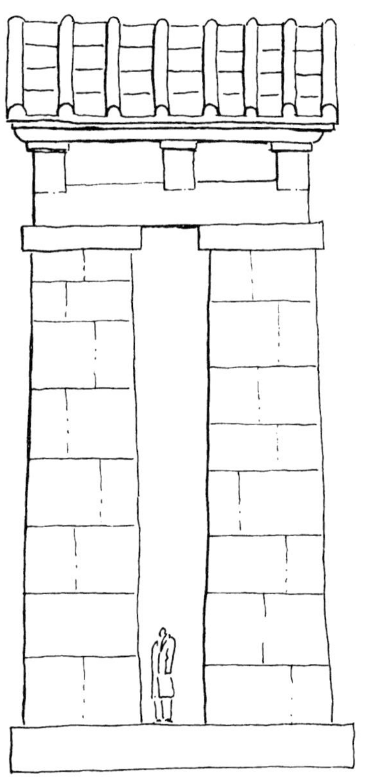

MIDGET
"monument"

vernacular scale
MONUMENTAL RETHORIC

EFFETE

PRETENTIOUS
INAPPROPRIATE

MINIATURE

Architecture

MONSTER
"SHED"

monumental scale
VERNACULAR PROSE

GROSS

POMPOUS
WEAK

MONUMENTALIST

BUILDING

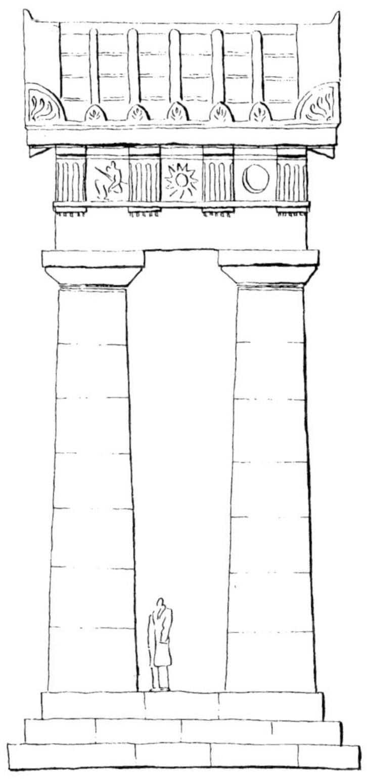

HUMAN DIMENSIONS
DOMESTIC SCALE
TECTONIC LOGIC
ARTISANAL
"MATERIALOGICAL"
TECHNOLOGICAL
MIMESIS
RES PRIVATA
Building

SUPERHUMAN DIMENSIONS
MONUMENTAL SCALE
ARCHITECTONIC LOGIC
ARTISTIC
"MATERIALOGICAL"
SYMBOLIC
ENCODED MIMESIS
RES PUBLICA
ARCHITECTURE

BULIMIC
CLASSICAL
ANOREXIC

CLASSICAL PROPORTIONS DISTORTED ↕ + ↔

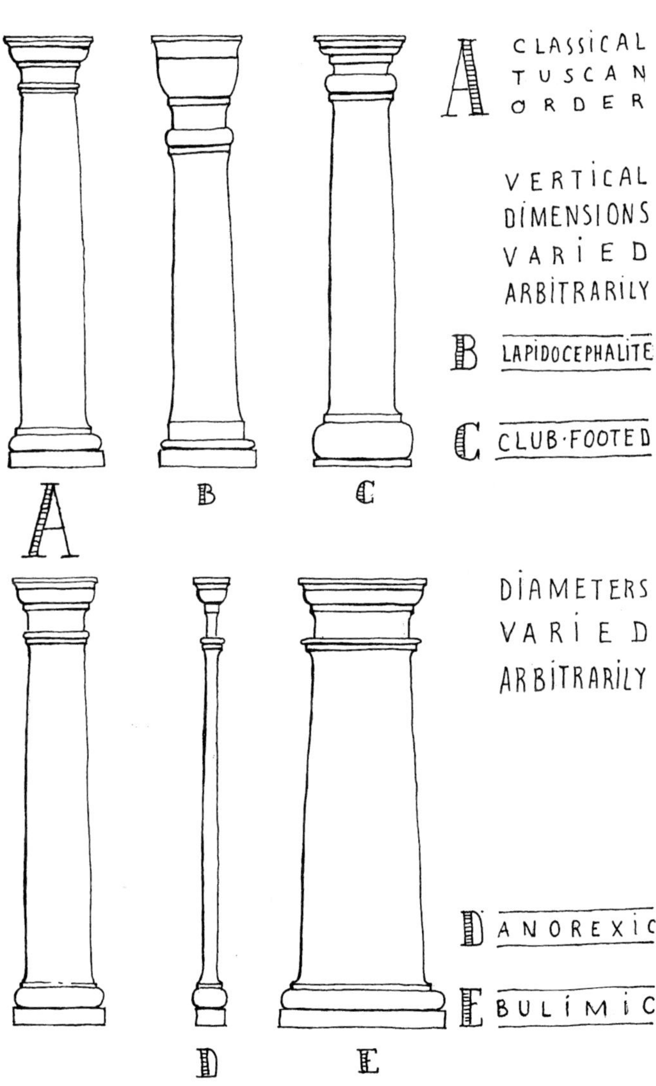

something went wrong

ON THE BUILDING SITE

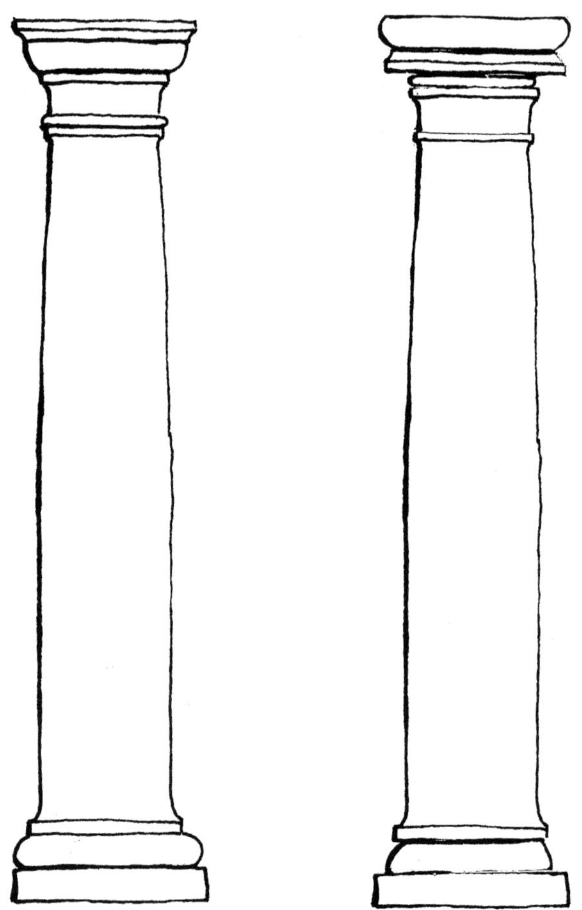

"Not to worry ~ Nobody will see the difference"

CLASSICAL

ACLASSICAL

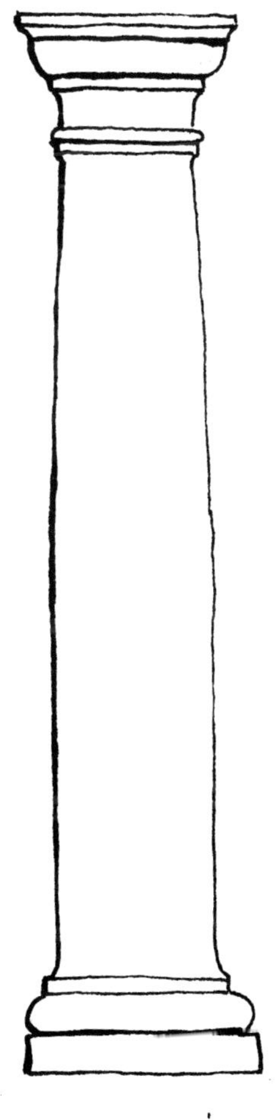

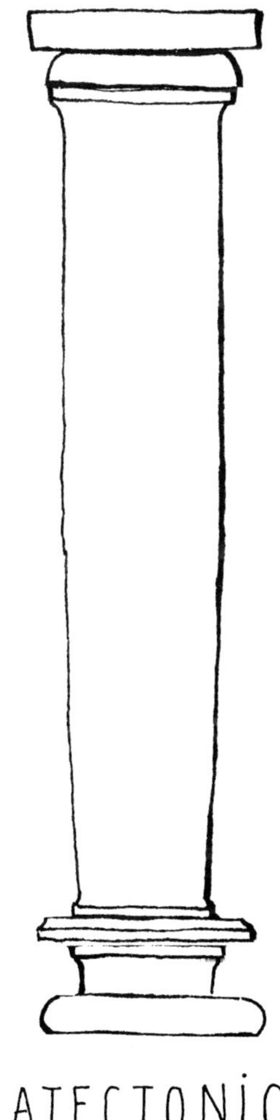

TECTONIC
PARTS MARRIED

ATECTONIC
PARTS DIVORCED

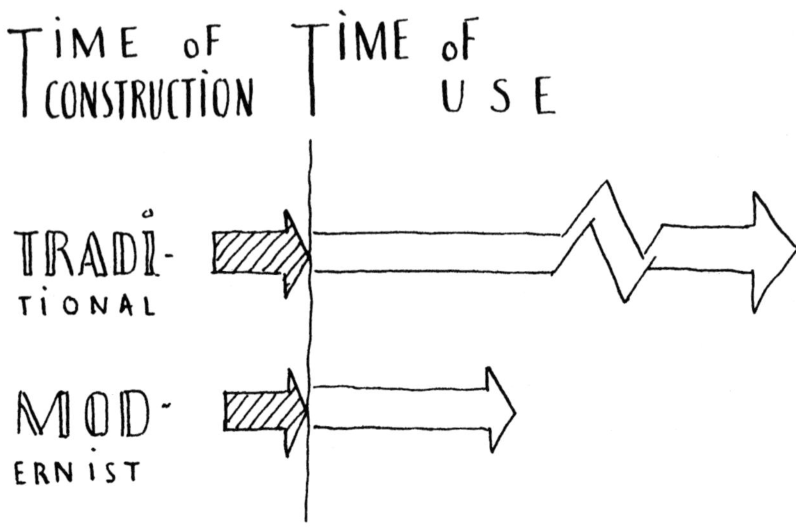

THE SOCIAL EFFICIENCY OF A BUILDING-METHOD IS MEASURED BY RELATING A BUILDING'S TIME OF USE TO ITS TIME OF CONSTRUCTION

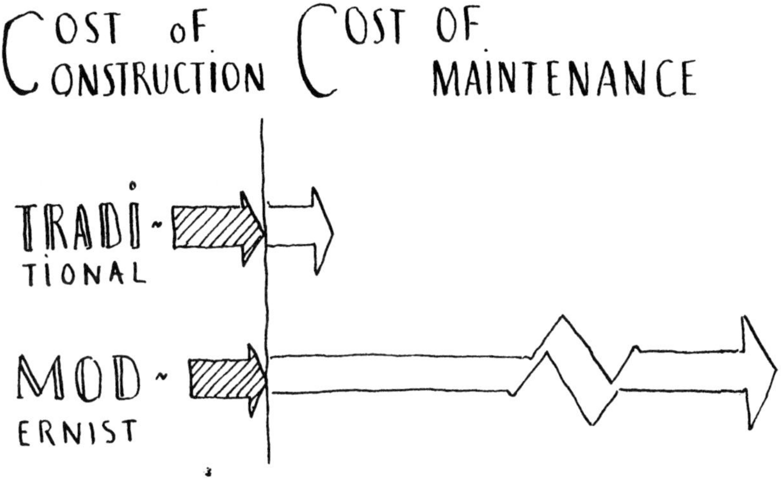

COST OF CONSTRUCTION | COST OF MAINTENANCE

TRADI~TIONAL

MOD~ERNIST

THE ECOLOGICAL AND ECONOMIC COST-EFFICIENCY OF A BUILDING METHOD IS MEASURED BY DIVIDING THE ADDED COST OF CONSTRUCTION AND LONG-TERM MAINTENANCE BY THE NUMBER OF USE~YEARS

TRADITIONAL versus MODERNIST MODES of CONSTRUCTION

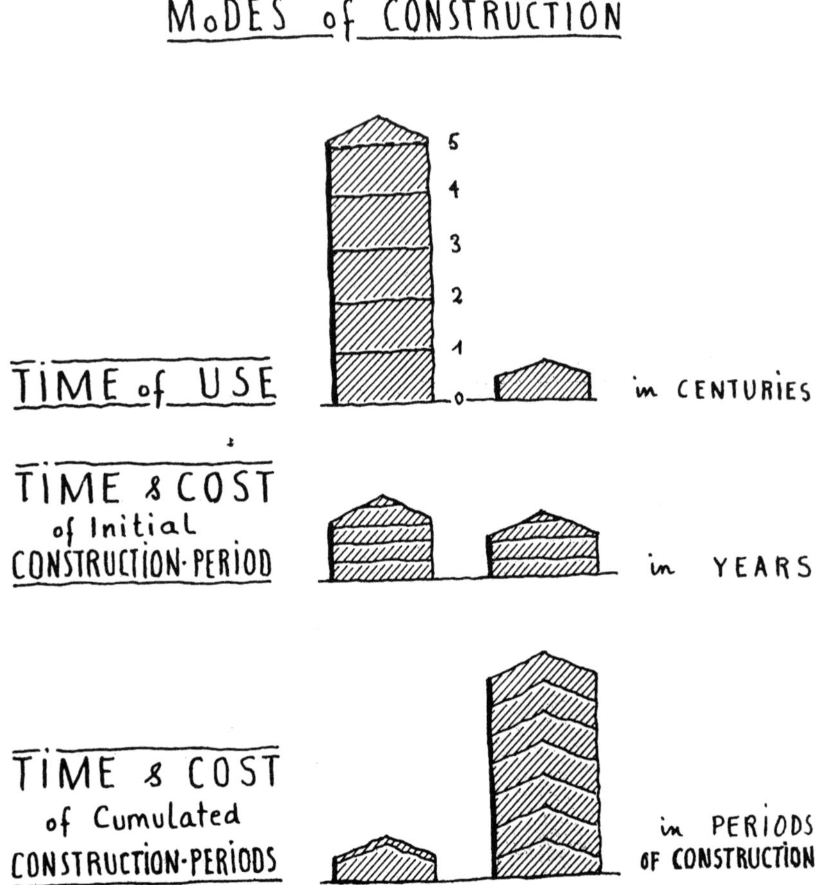

TRADITIONAL MODERNIST

THE 6TH ORDER
OR
THE END OF ARCHITECTURE
L.K. 77

CONSTRUCTIONAL MONISM & STYLISTIC PLURALISM

UNITY OF CONSTRUCTION CULTURE

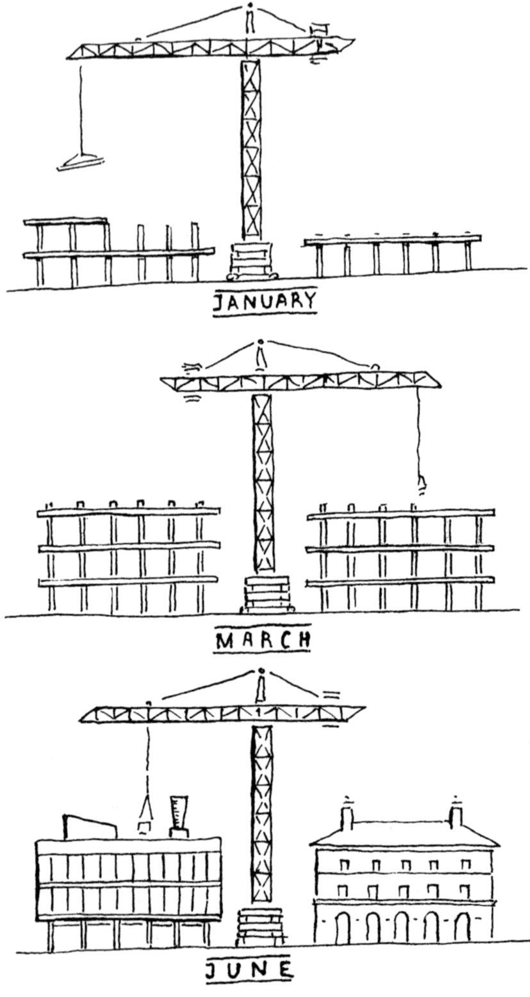

LAST MINUTE SURPRISE ON BUILDING - SITE
LK 84

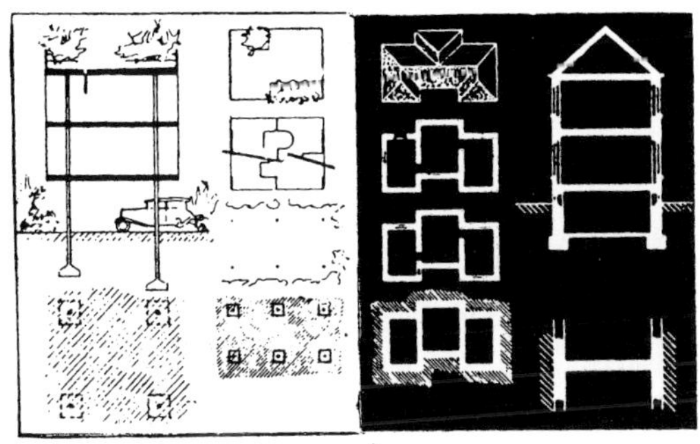

LE CORBUSIER
5 POINTS OF A NEW ARCHITECTURE
AGAINST TRADITIONAL BUILDING

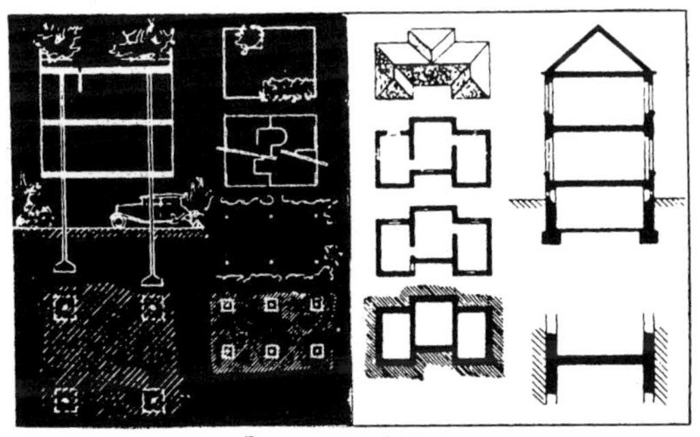

LÉON KRIER
5 POINTS OF TRADITIONAL BUILDING

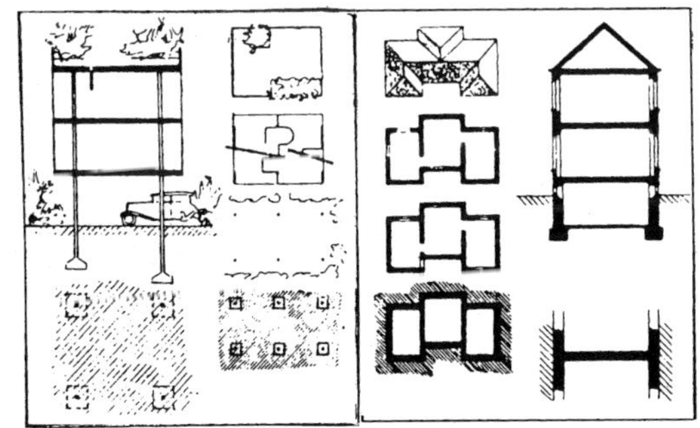

10 POINTS OF PRESENT BUILDING

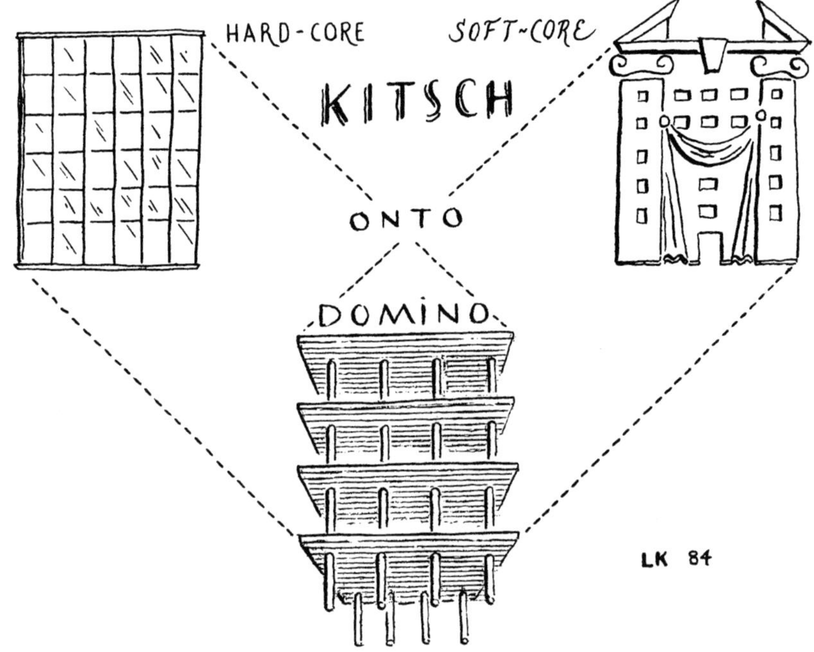

Plus ça change, plus c'est la même chose

DISTANCE & DETAIL

I am a house

call me a house

I am a window

call me a window

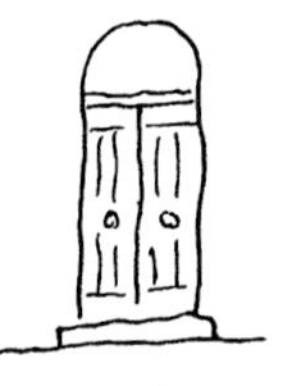

I am a house-door

call me a house-door

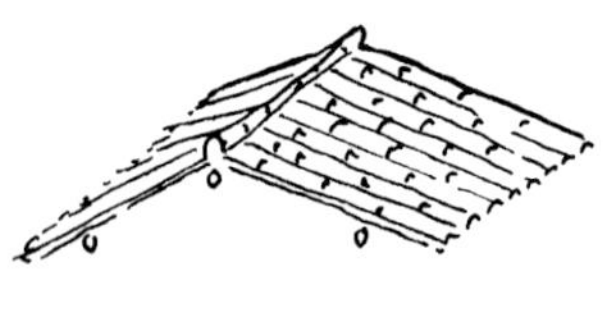

I am a roof

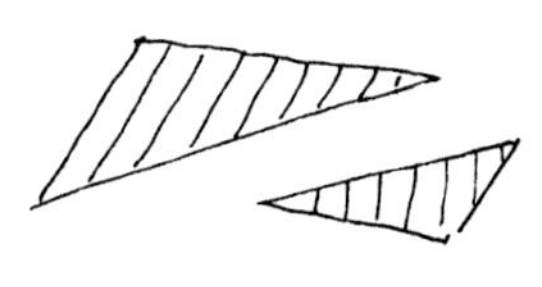

call me a roof

LK 82

I AM A LINTEL
I AM A SHUTTER
I AM A MASONRY WALL
I AM A WINDOW
I AM AN ARCHIVOLT
I AM A FAN-LIGHT
I AM A STONE WALL
I AM A PLINTH
CALL ME A A "LINTEL"
CALL ME A "SHUTTER"
CALL ME A "MASONRY WALL"
CALL ME A "WINDOW"
CALL ME AN "ARCHIVOLT"
CALL A "FAN-LIGHT"
CALL ME A "STONEWALL
CALL ME A "PLINTH"
I AM A HOUSE
NATURAL MATERIALS
AUTHENTIC TRADITIONAL
CALL ME A "HOUSE"
SYNTHETIC MATERIALS
"TRADITIONALIST" KITSCH

PROPORTIONAL HARMONISATION OF VOLUMES AND VOIDS

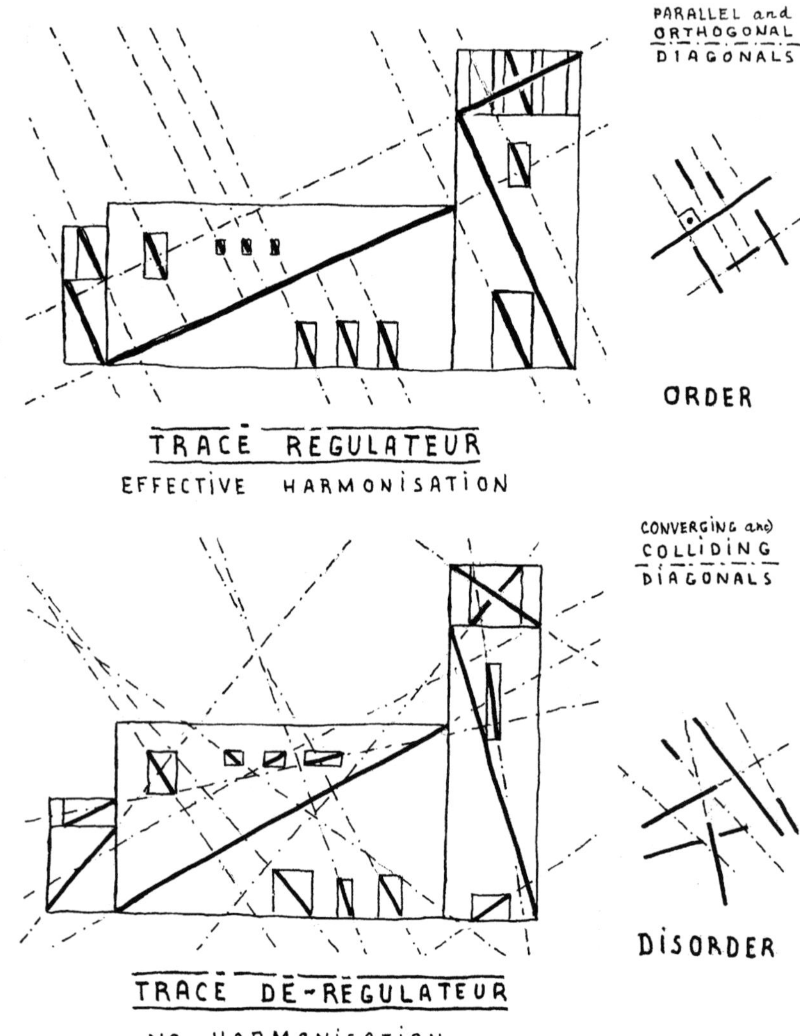

CITY / ANTI-CITY: URBS VERSUS SUBURBIA

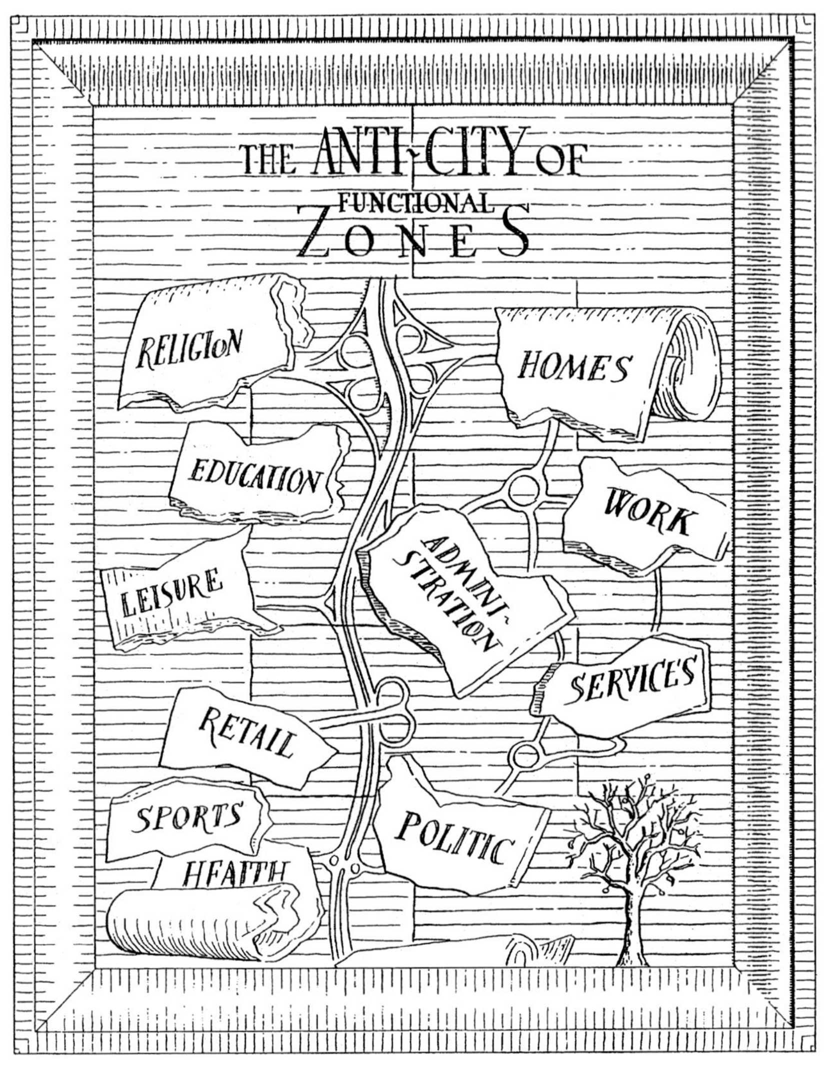
THE ANTI-CITY OF
FUNCTIONAL
ZONES
RELIGION
HOMES
EDUCATION
WORK
ADMINI-
STRATION
LEISURE
SERVICES
RETAIL
SPORTS
POLITIC
HEALTH

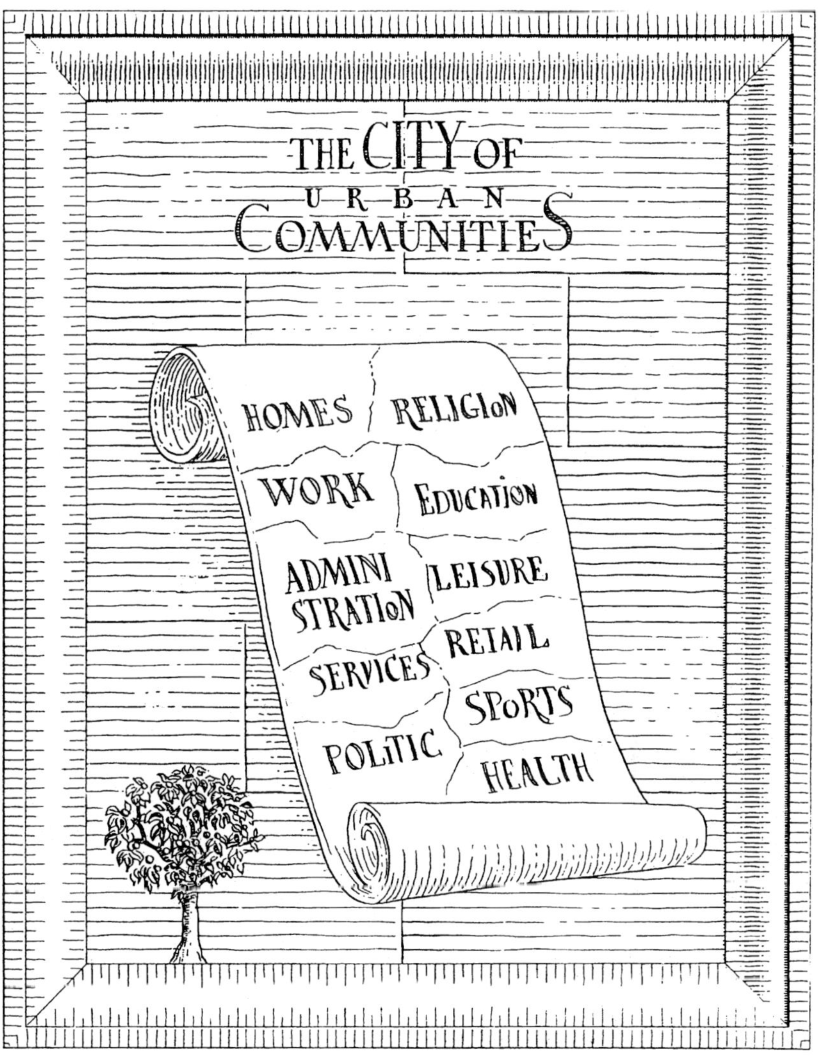
THE CITY OF
URBAN
COMMUNITIES
HOMES
RELIGION
WORK
EDUCATION
ADMINI STRATION
LEISURE
RETAIL
SERVICES
SPORTS
POLITIC
HEALTH

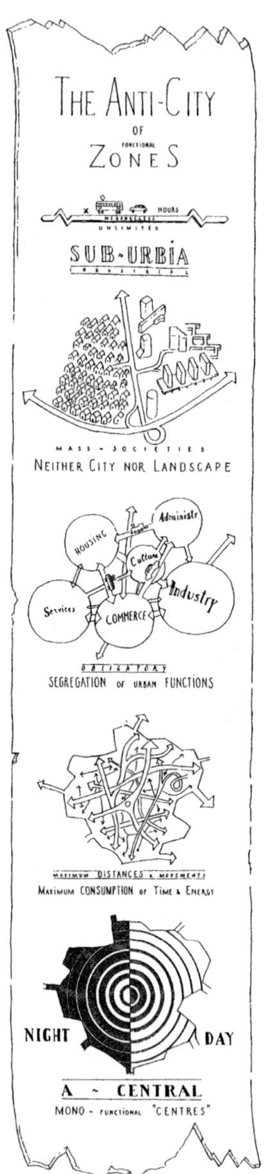
THE ANTI-CITY
OF
FUNCTIONAL
ZONES
HOURS
UNLIMITED
SUB-URBIA
INDUSTRIAL
MASS-SOCIETIES
NEITHER CITY NOR LANDSCAPE
HOUSING
Administr
Culture
Industry
Services
COMMERCE
OBLIGATORY
SEGREGATION OF URBAN FUNCTIONS
MAXIMUM DISTANCES & MOVEMENTS
MAXIMUM CONSUMPTION OF TIME & ENERGY
NIGHT
DAY
A - CENTRAL
MONO-FUNCTIONAL "CENTRES"

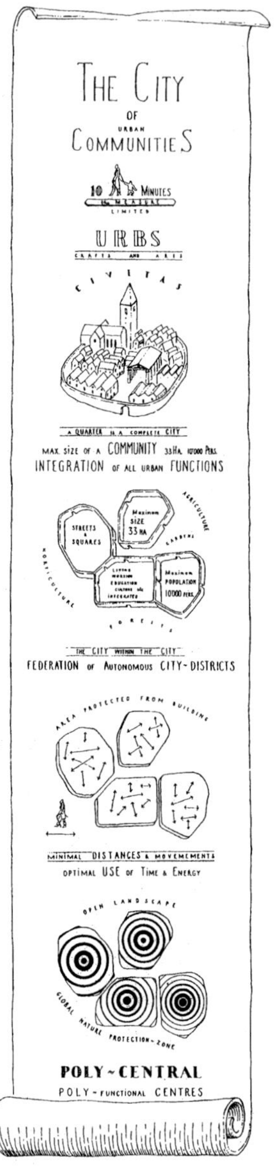
THE CITY
OF
URBAN
COMMUNITIES
10 MINUTES
LIMITED
URBS
CRAFTS AND ARTS
CIVITAS
A QUARTER IS A COMPLETE CITY
MAX. SIZE OF A COMMUNITY 33HA 10000 PERS.
INTEGRATION OF ALL URBAN FUNCTIONS
STREETS & SQUARES
Maximum SIZE 33 HA
Maximum POPULATION 10000 PERS.
AGRICULTURE
GARDENS
HORTICULTURE
FORESTS
THE CITY WITHIN THE CITY
FEDERATION OF AUTONOMOUS CITY-DISTRICTS
AREA PROTECTED FROM BUILDING
MINIMAL DISTANCES & MOVEMENTS
OPTIMAL USE OF TIME & ENERGY
OPEN LANDSCAPE
GLOBAL NATURE PROTECTION-ZONE
POLY-CENTRAL
POLY-FUNCTIONAL CENTRES

CITY

VARIABLE NUMBER

OF

COMPLETE
URBAN COMMUNITIES

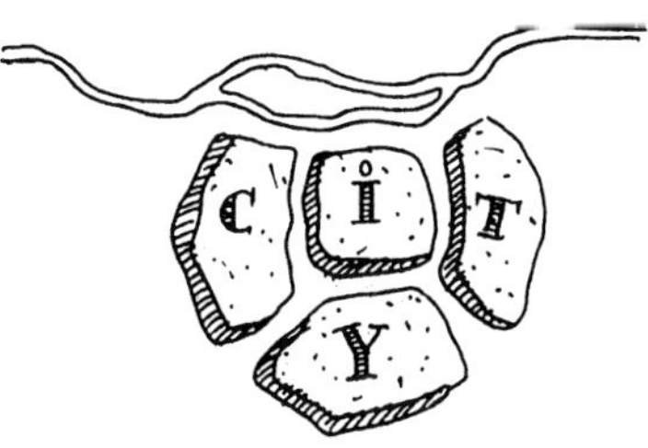

ANTI-CITY

VARIABLE NUMBER

OF

MONO-FUNCTIONAL
ZONES

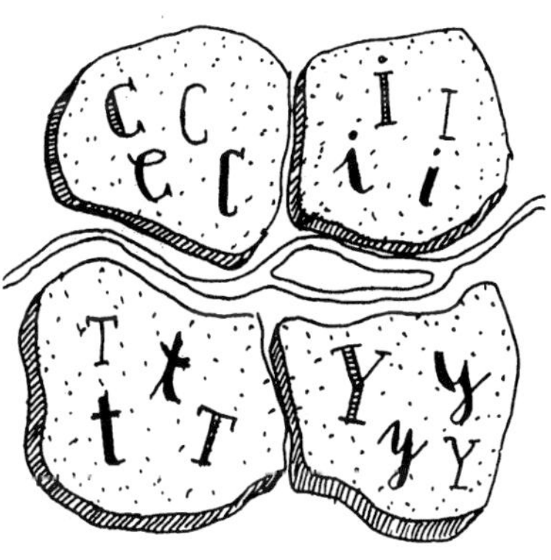

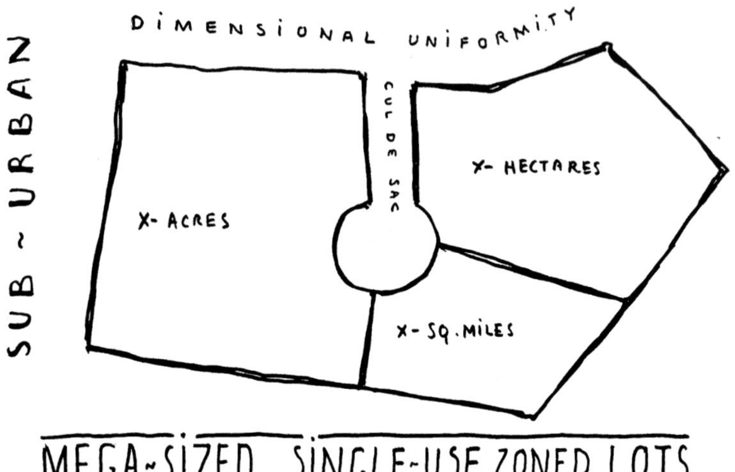

MEGA-SIZED SINGLE-USE ZONED LOTS

SOCIAL, FUNCTIONAL AND ARCHITECTURAL
MONOTONY

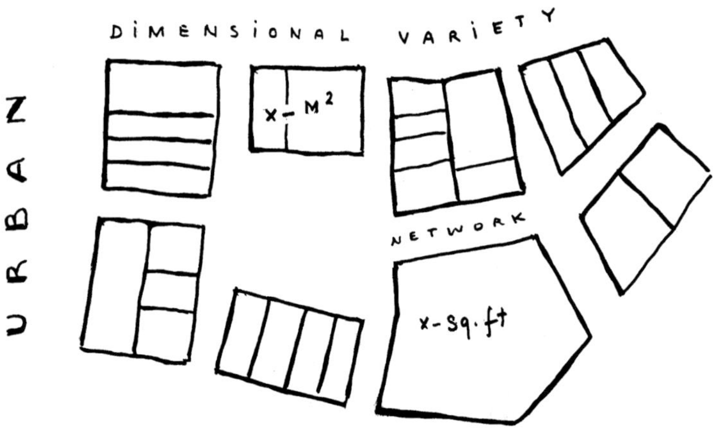

VARIOUSLY SIZED + USED BUILDING LOTS

SOCIAL, FUNCTIONAL + ARCHITECTURAL
VARIETY

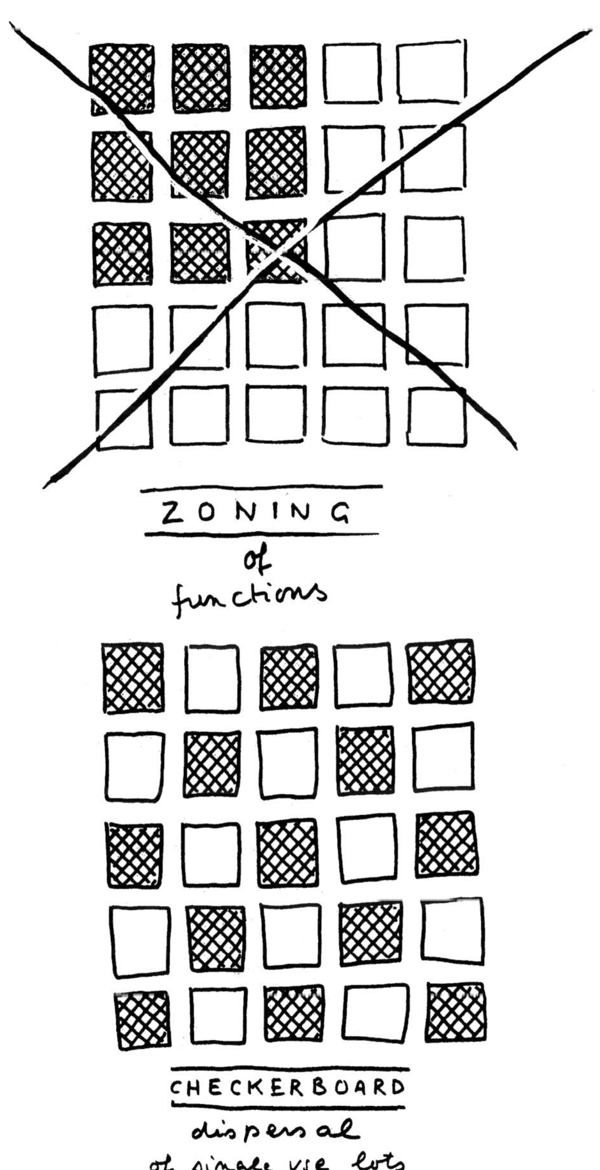
ZONING
of
functions
CHECKERBOARD
dispersal
of single use lots

SETBACKS ENFORCE BUILDING AWAY FROM PLOT~ BOUNDARY

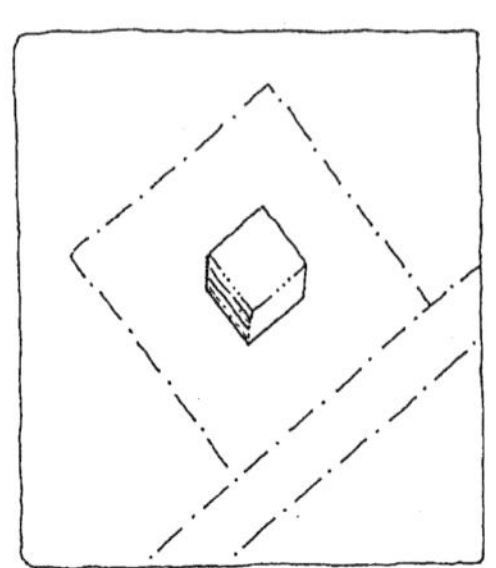

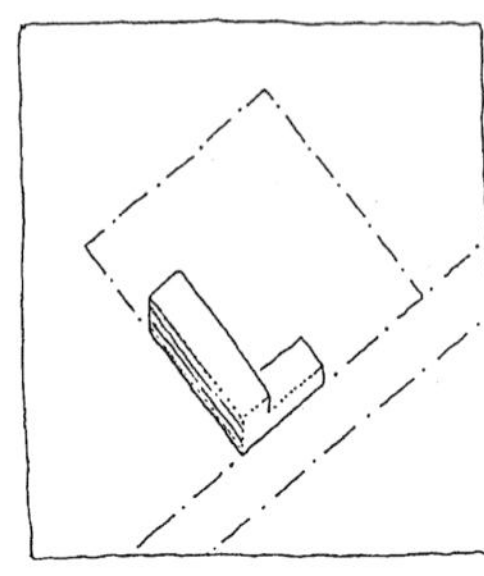

ALIGNEMENTS ENFORCE BUILDING ON The BOUNDARY OF THE PLOT

ONLY REALIZING A WEAK DIFFERENCI~ ATION OF PRIVATE AND PUBLIC REALM

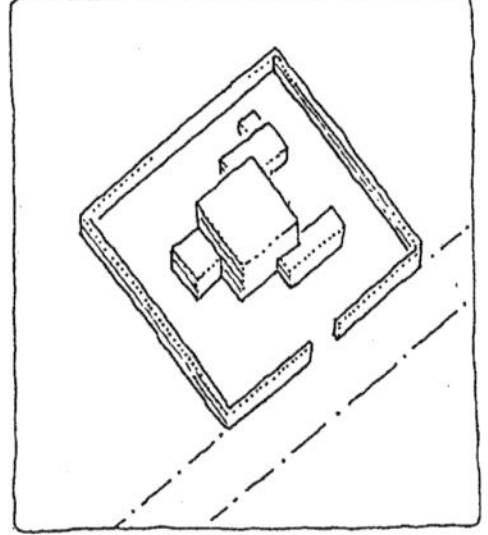

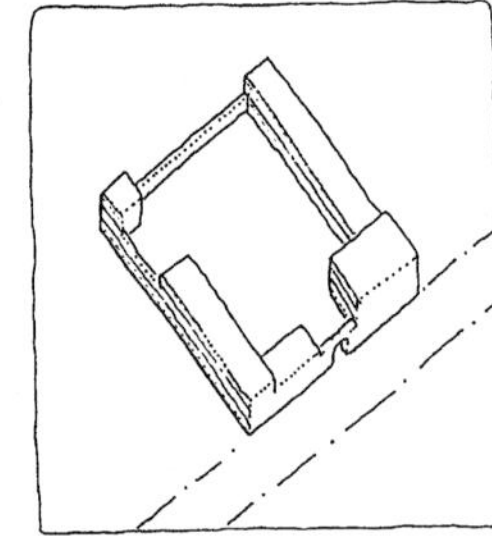

FRONTAGES ESTABLISH A PHYSICAL DISTINCTION BETWEEN PUBLIC AND PRIVATE REALM

URBAN GROWTH INCREASES THE FEELING OF DISORDER OF THE ENVIRONMENT

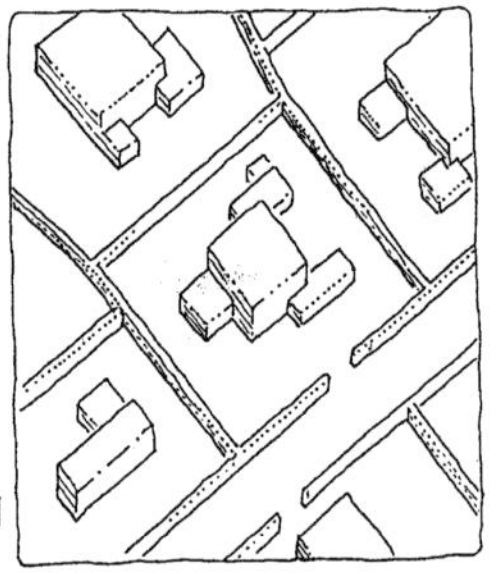

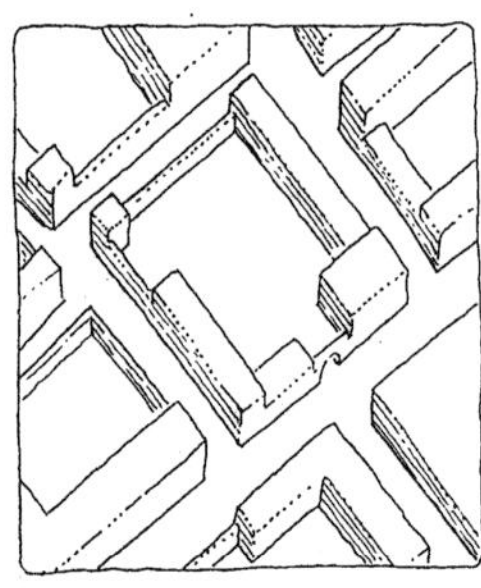

URBAN GROWTH INCREASES THE FEELING OF ORDER AND URBANITY

SUB~URBAN

URBAN

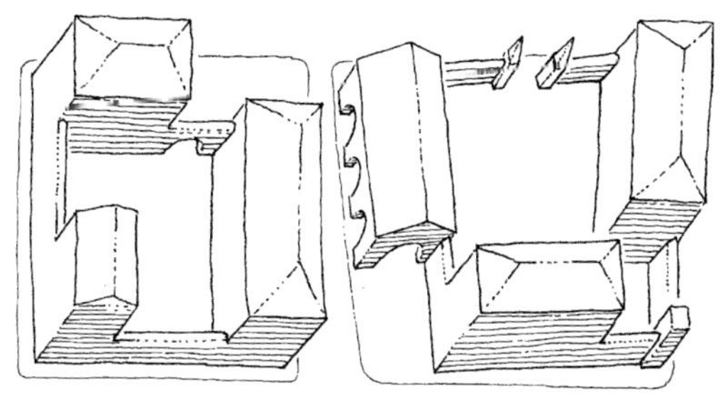

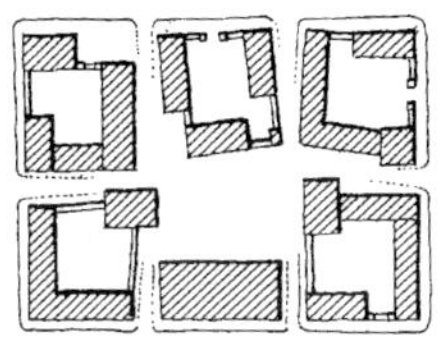

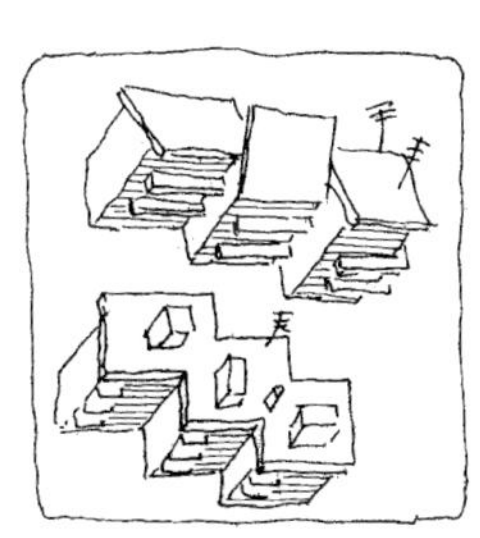

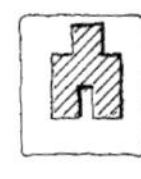

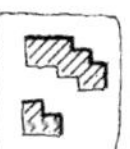

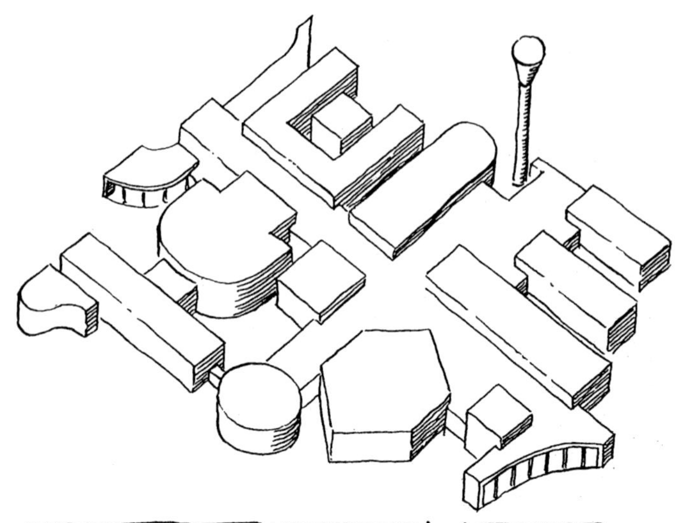

CONCENTRATION OF CIVIC USES

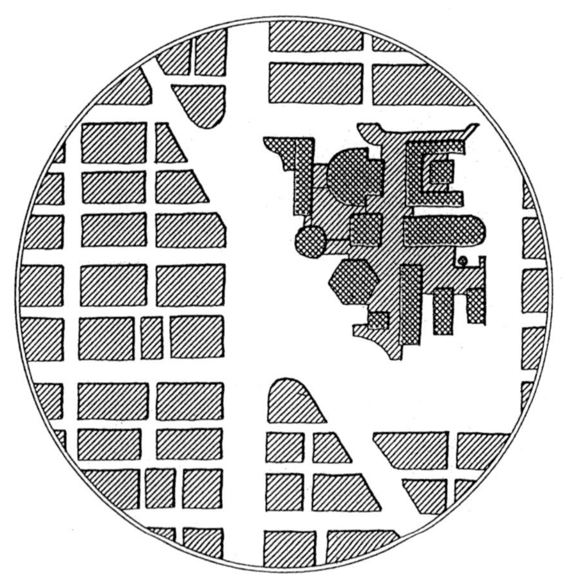

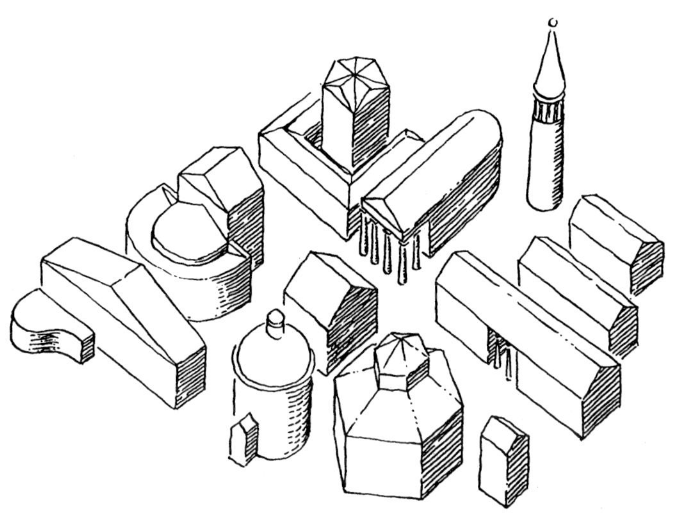

DISPERSAL OF CIVIC USES

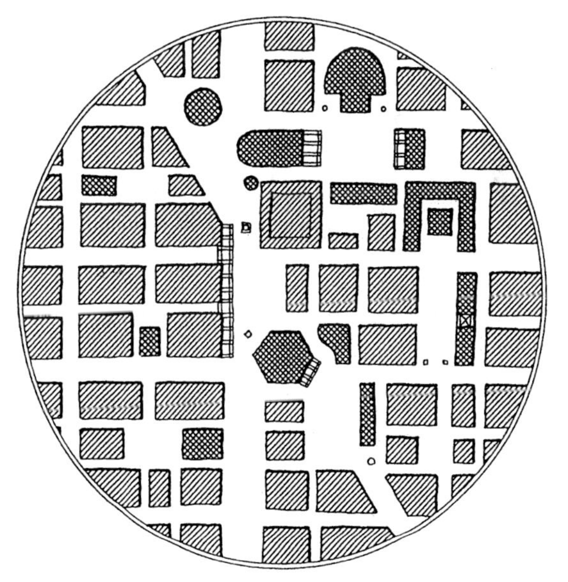

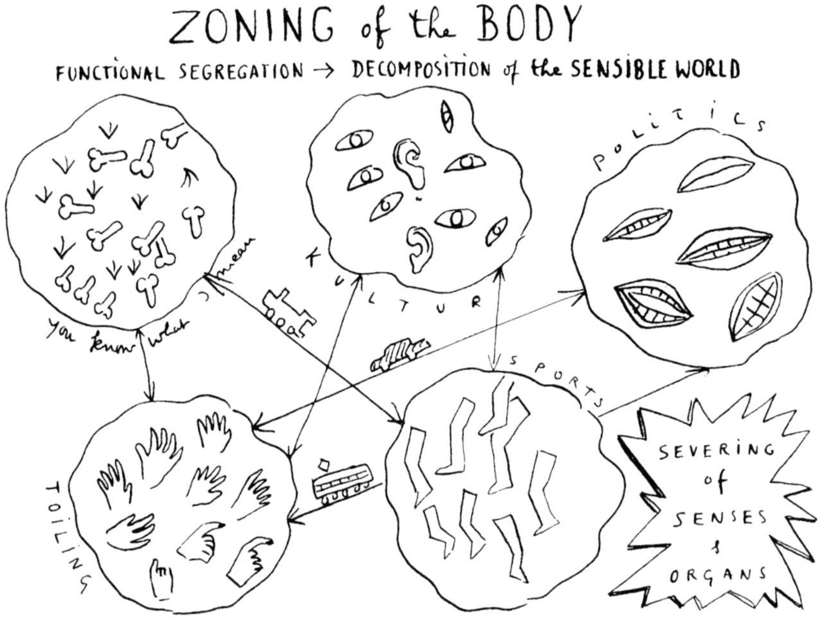

ZONING of the BODY

FUNCTIONAL SEGREGATION → DECOMPOSITION of the SENSIBLE WORLD

you know what I mean

KULTUR

POLITICS

SPORTS

TOILING

SEVERING of SENSES & ORGANS

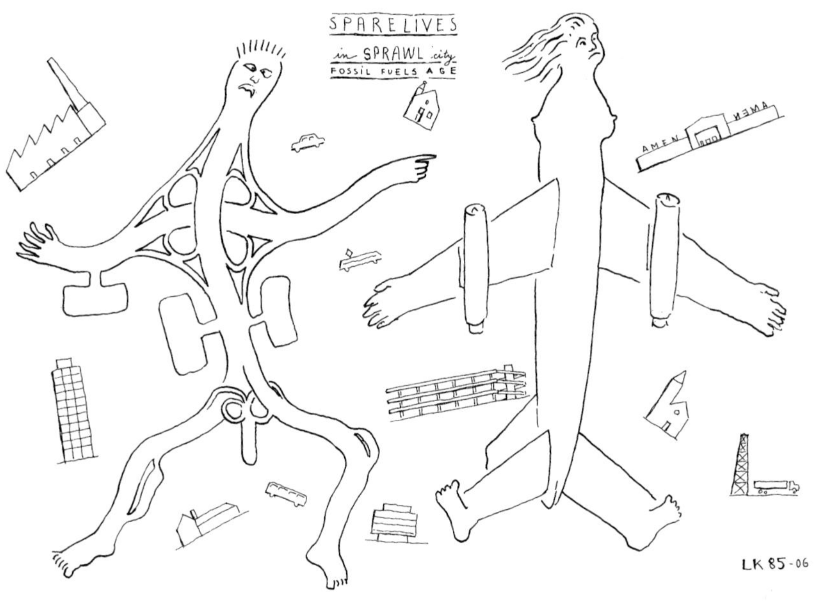
SPARE LIVES
in SPRAWL city
FOSSIL FUELS AGE
AMEN
AMEN
LK 85-06

The Idea of "Zoning"

as applied to the weekly gastronomical intake of an individual of the human species

WORLD CENTRAL COMMITTEE DIRECTIVE N° 1

monday ~ 32 Pints of Liquids ....

Tuesday ~ 3 Kg of Meat ....

Wednesday ~ 2,5 Kg of Fats ....

Thursday ~ 3 Kg of Pasta ....

Friday ~ 2 Kg of Fish ....

Saturday ~ 6 Pints of alcoolic Drinks ....

Sunday ~ 6 ℔ of Backery ....

mond........ Note Individual deceased .... Experiment discontinued

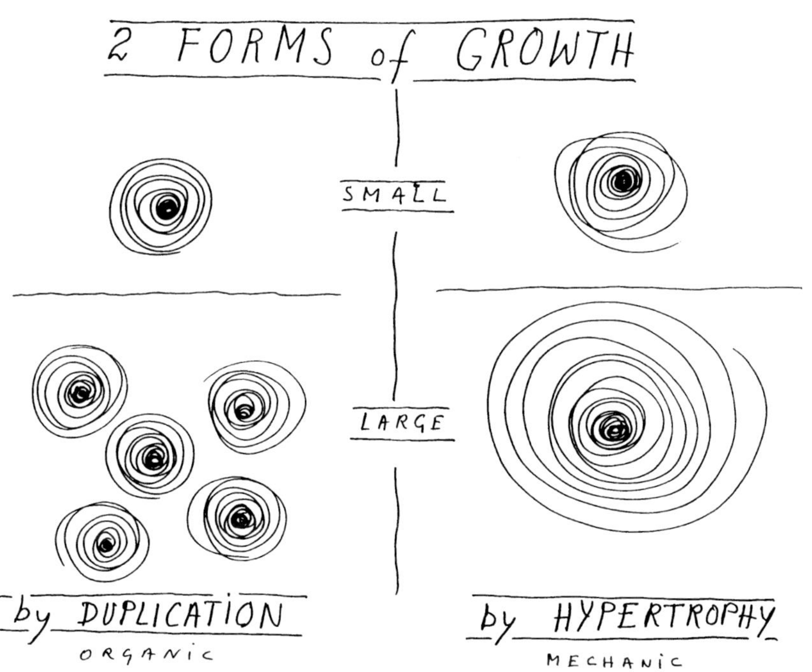
2 FORMS of GROWTH
SMALL
LARGE
by DUPLICATION
ORGANIC
by HYPERTROPHY
MECHANIC

A FUNCTIONAL ZONE
admits
one single quality (function) of a City
at the exclusion of all others

All that is not specifically obligatory is strictly forbidden

An URBAN QUARTER
CONtains and PROmotes
all the Qualities of a
CITY

IN-CLUSIVE

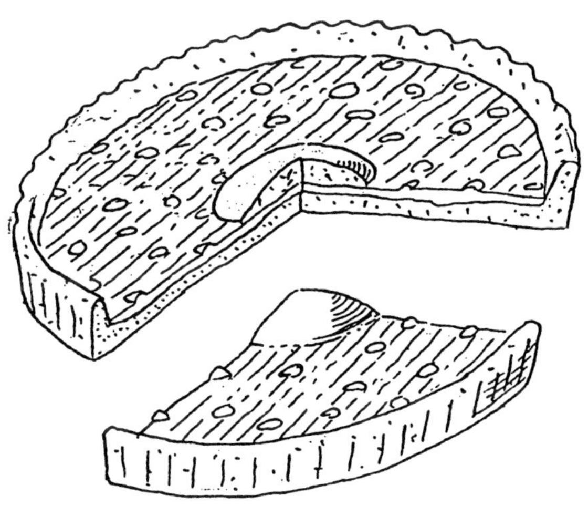

All is Permitted & Promoted
that is not strictly forbidden

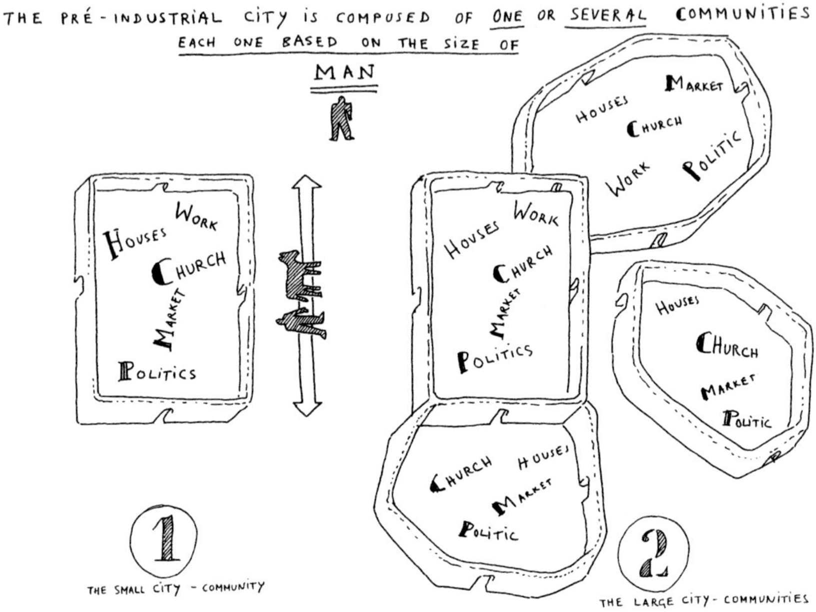

THE PRÉ-INDUSTRIAL CITY IS COMPOSED OF ONE OR SEVERAL COMMUNITIES EACH ONE BASED ON THE SIZE OF

MAN

HOUSES WORK
CHURCH
MARKET
POLITICS

1

THE SMALL CITY - COMMUNITY

HOUSES MARKET
CHURCH
WORK POLITIC

HOUSES WORK
CHURCH
MARKET
POLITICS

HOUSES
CHURCH
MARKET
POLITIC

CHURCH HOUSES
MARKET
POLITIC

2

THE LARGE CITY - COMMUNITIES

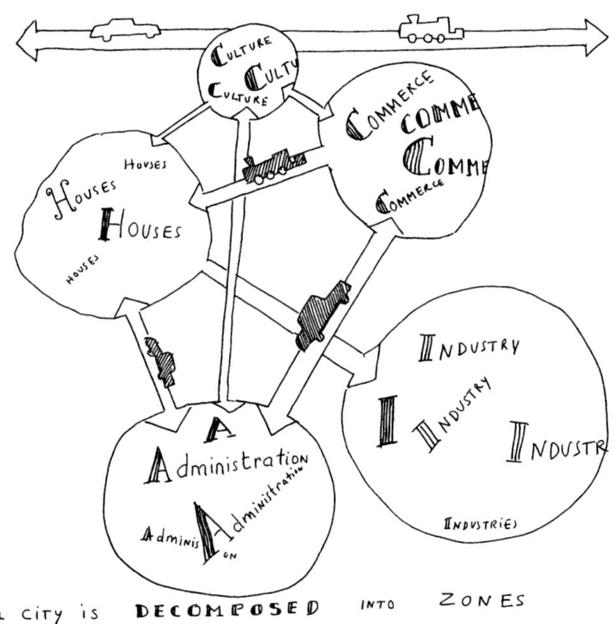

THE INDUSTRIAL CITY IS **DECOMPOSED** INTO ZONES

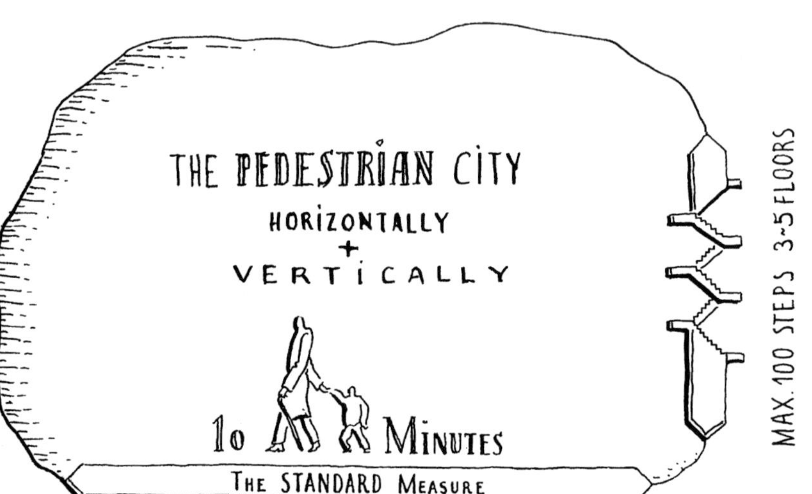
THE PEDESTRIAN CITY
HORIZONTALLY
+
VERTICALLY
10 MINUTES
THE STANDARD MEASURE
WALKING
MAX. 100 STEPS 3–5 FLOORS

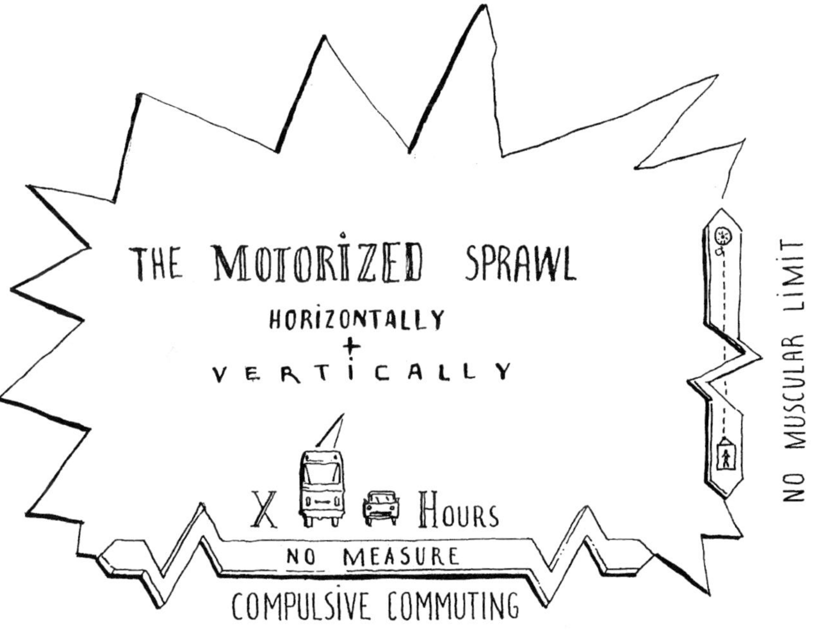
THE MOTORIZED SPRAWL
HORIZONTALLY
+
VERTICALLY
X
HOURS
NO MEASURE
COMPULSIVE COMMUTING
NO MUSCULAR LIMIT

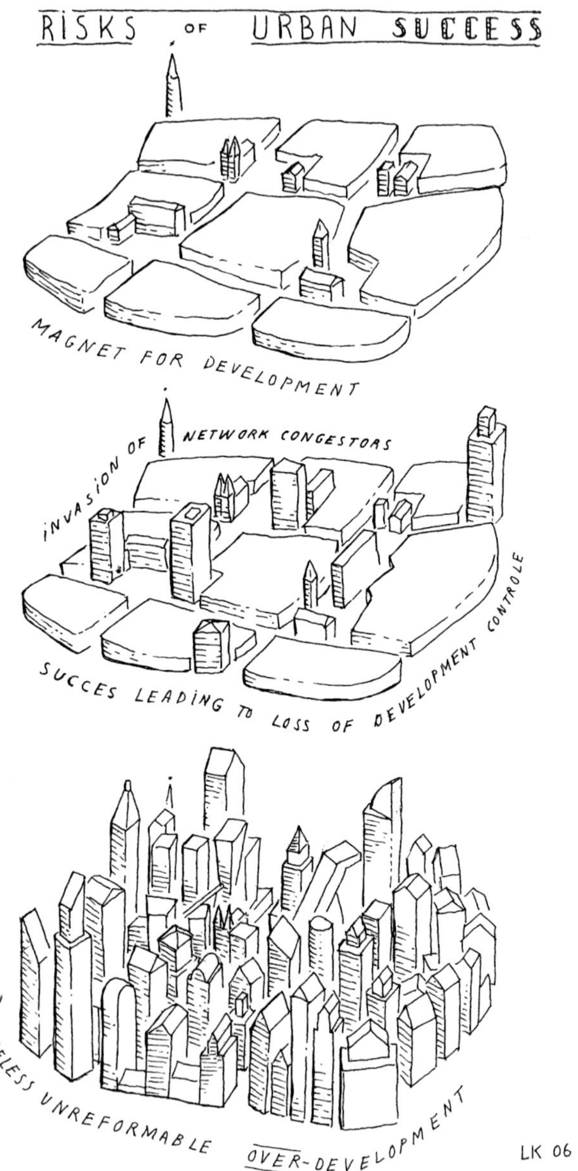
RISKS OF URBAN SUCCESS
MAGNET FOR DEVELOPMENT
INVASION OF NETWORK CONGESTORS
SUCCES LEADING TO LOSS OF DEVELOPMENT CONTROLE
FUTURELESS UNREFORMABLE OVER-DEVELOPMENT
LK 06

VERTICAL & HORIZONTAL

URBAN GROWTHS and CONGESTORS

GROWTH · HYPERGROWTH · WEEDS ETC

MATURE
HORIZONTAL NETWORK
WITH VERTICAL PEDESTRIAN
TWIGS (SHORT CUL-DE-SACS)

MATURE
HORIZONTAL NETWORK
USURPED BY OVERSIZED MECHANIZED
CUL-DE-SACS (WEEDS)
NETWORK CONGESTORS

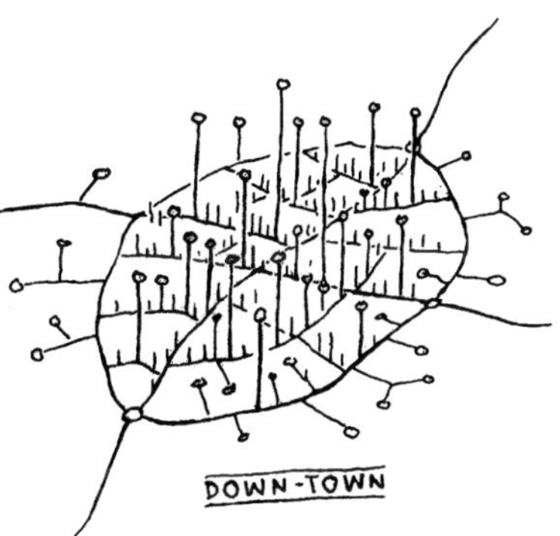

SPRAWL

SPRAWLING LABYRINTH
MECHANIZED VERTICAL AND
HORIZONTAL CUL-DE-SACS · MAXIMUM
GEOGRAPHIC CONGESTION

ANTIURBAN LABYRINTH

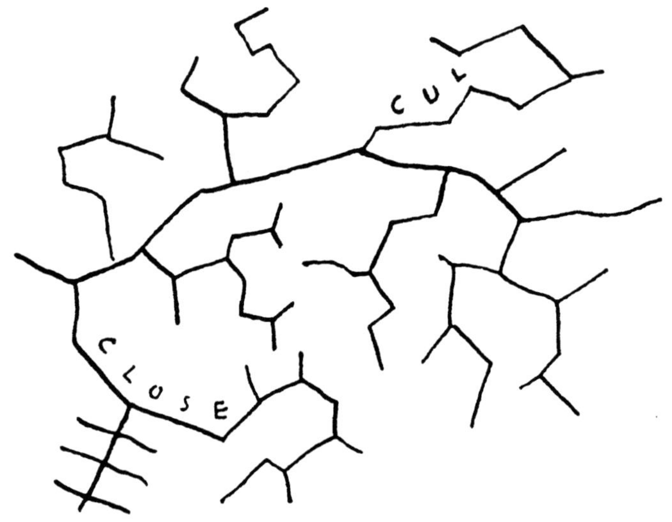

SUB~URB

FAU~BOURG

BAN~LIEU

VOR~ORT

TRABANTEN~STADT

TOWNSHIP

SATELLITE

THE ARSE OF THE WORLD

URBAN PATTERN

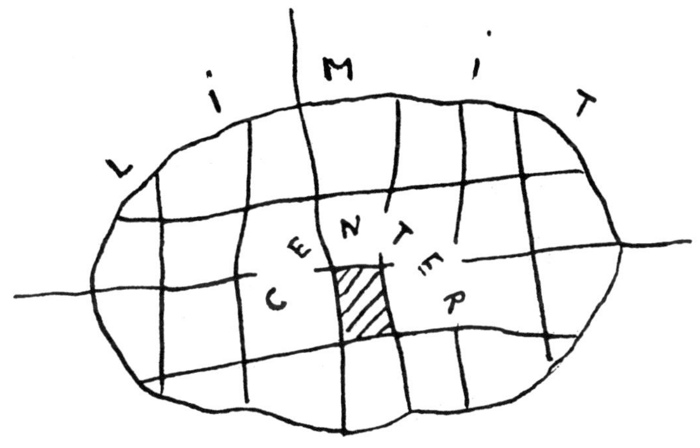

URBS

BOURG

LIEU

ORT

STADT

TOWN

CITY

CENTER OF THE WORLD

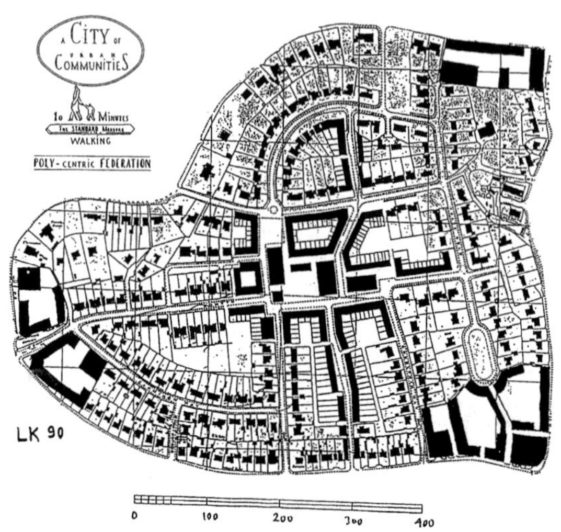

REDEVELOPMENT through FUNCTIONAL and TYPOLOGICAL MIX

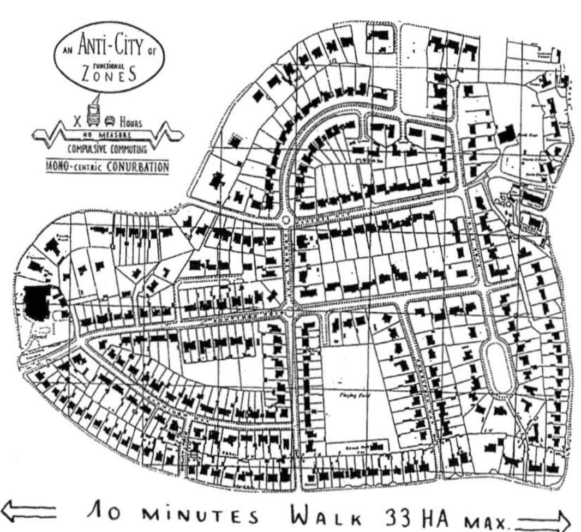

⟸ 10 MINUTES WALK 33 HA MAX. ⟹

TYPICAL SEGMENT OF 100% RESIDENTIAL SUBURB

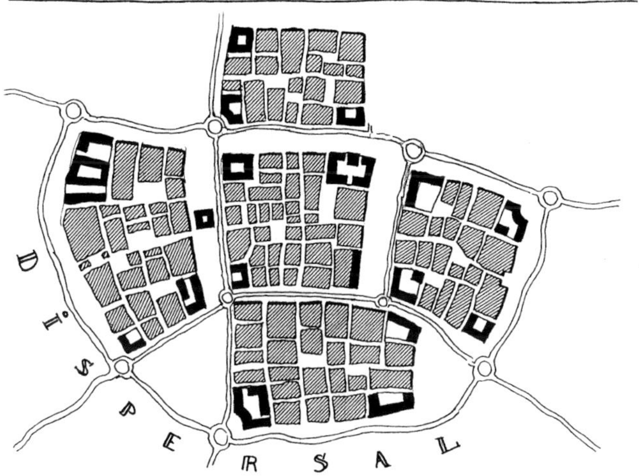
CORRECT ZONING OF LARGE EMPLOYMENT
DISPERSAL

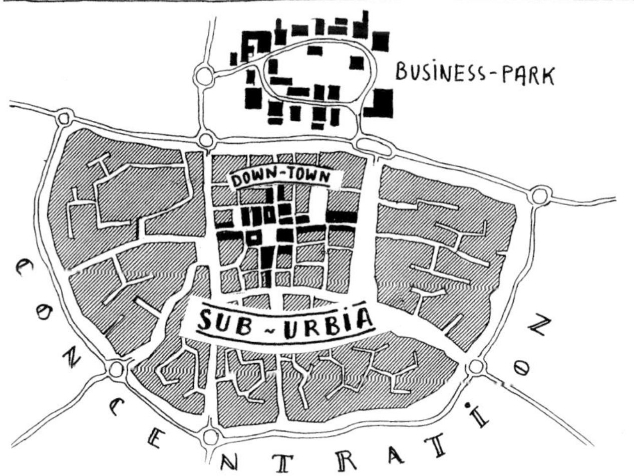
MISTAKEN ZONING OF LARGE EMPLOYMENT
BUSINESS-PARK
DOWN-TOWN
SUB-URBIA
CONCENTRATION

The CITY as COMMUNITY(IES)

CULTURAL, POLITICAL, ECONOMICAL

RELIGIOUS ⇒ RELIGATA

The CITY	The BIG CITY
COMMUNITY CIVITAS PARISH etc	FEDERATIO of COMMUNITIES etc

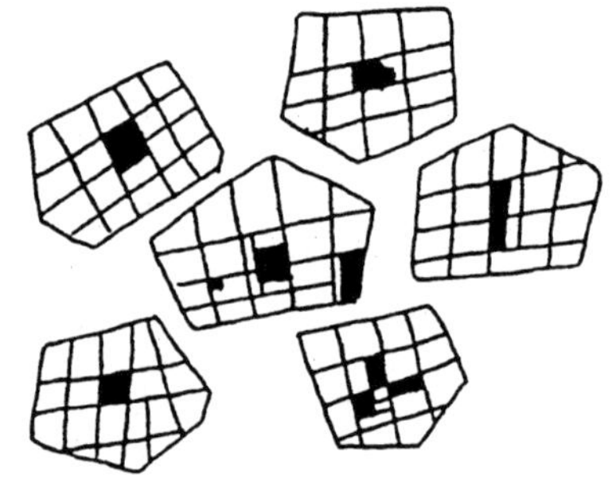

MONO-CENTRIC

POLY-CENTRIC

10 MINUTES

N x 10 MINUTES

The CITY'S LIMIT is a BUILT one

The INDUSTRIAL Anti-CITY

A - CENTRIC

ANTI-URBAN - ANTI-RURAL

UNLIMITED EXPANSION

The CITY'S LIMIT is an ADMINISTRATIVE LINE

The CITY of the PEDESTRIAN

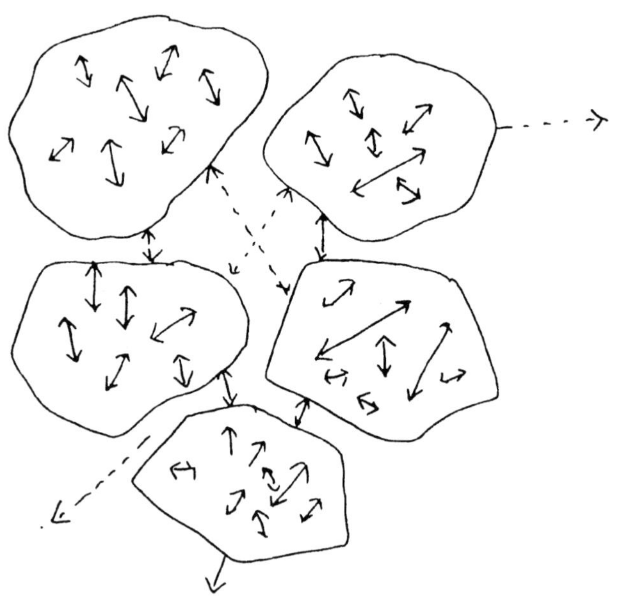

MINIMUM DISTANCES
FOR MAXIMUM ACHIEVEMENT & PLEASURE

The (Anti-) CITY of the MOTORCAR

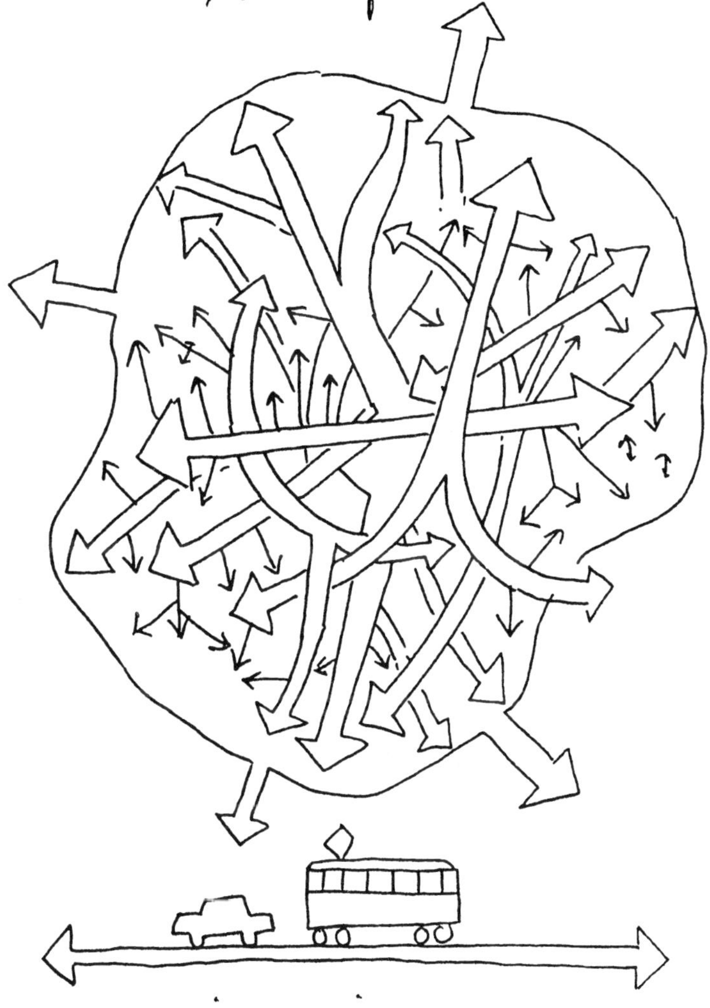

MAXIMUM DISTANCES
AND BOREDOM for MINIMUM ACHIEVEMENT

correct density and composition
= nameable CITY

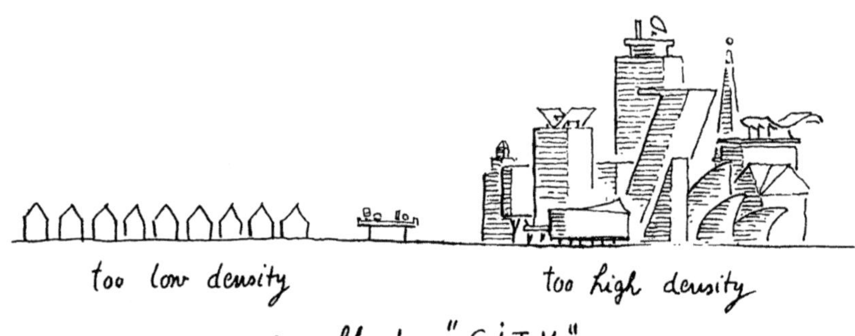

too low density — too high density
= socalled "CITY"

The City

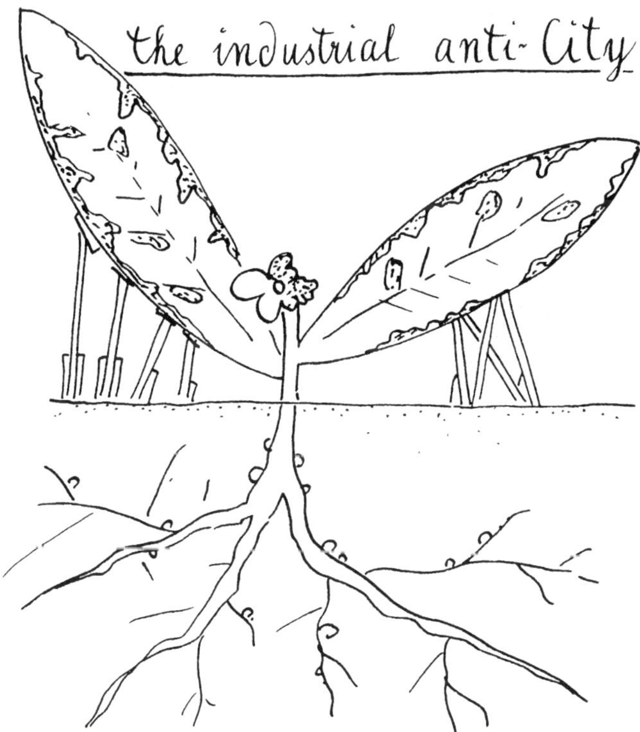

OVER-development of CENTER

UNJUSTIFIABLE PROFIT - MAKING

Urbanization of SUB-urb!

JUSTIFIED PROFIT MAKING

FUNDAMENTAL CHOICES OF URBAN DEVELOPMENT

the city

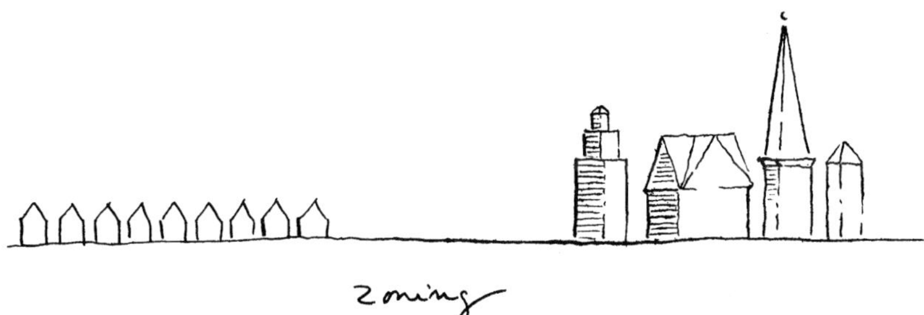
zoning

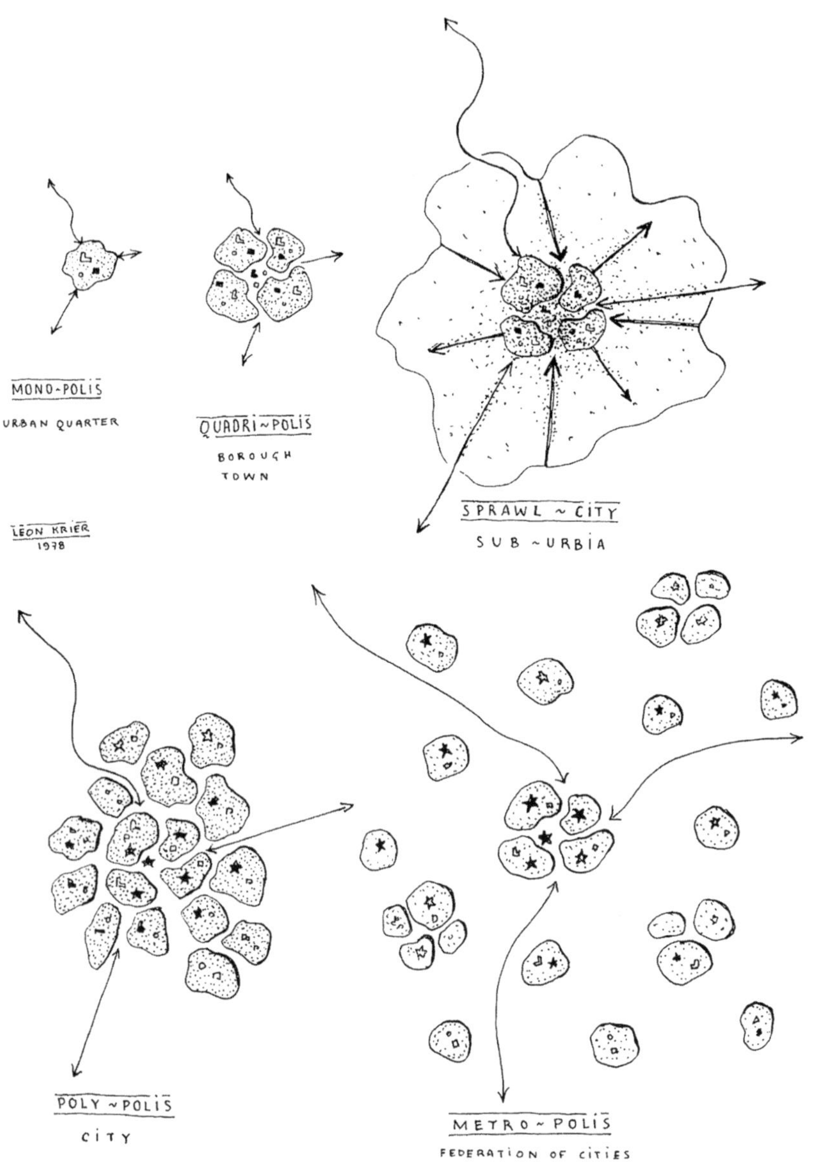
MONO~POLIS
URBAN QUARTER
QUADRI~POLIS
BOROUGH
TOWN
SPRAWL ~ CITY
SUB ~URBIA
LÉON KRIER
1978
POLY ~POLIS
CITY
METRO ~ POLIS
FEDERATION OF CITIES

CITY & PARASITE

CITY WITHOUT SUBURB

CITY WITH SUBURB

SUBURB WITHOUT CITY

CITIES WITHIN THE CITY

SUBurb no URBS ◦ BANlieu no LIEU ◦ FAUbourg no BOURG ◦ VORort no ORT

THE HANGMAN and its VICTIM
THE ANTI-CITY is out to KILL the CITY

CITY
and
LANDSCAPE
a good
MARIAGE

this City is no longer
a true CITY
this Landscape no longer
a true LANDSCAPE
SUBURB ALWAYS
DEFEATS BOTH

a SUBURB
WITHOUT a
CITY
WILL FIND ITS VICTIM
at whatever EXPENSE
EFFORT or DISTANCE

1850 ~ 1950

THE FORMATION of the INDUSTRIAL ANTI-CITY
(INDUSTRIAL CITY = CONTRADICTIO in TERMINI)

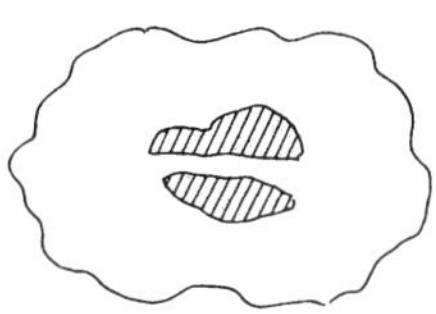

INDUSTRIAL
SUBURB ·
BANLIEU · FAUBOURG
VORORT ·
SATELLITES · TRABANTEN
BESIEGE
the CITY

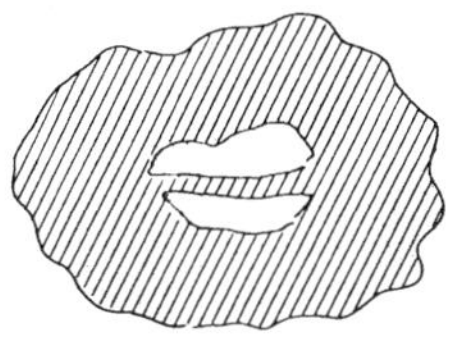

The CITY is
FINE
WITHOUT SUBURB

SUB~URB
UNTHINKABLE
WITHOUT the CITY

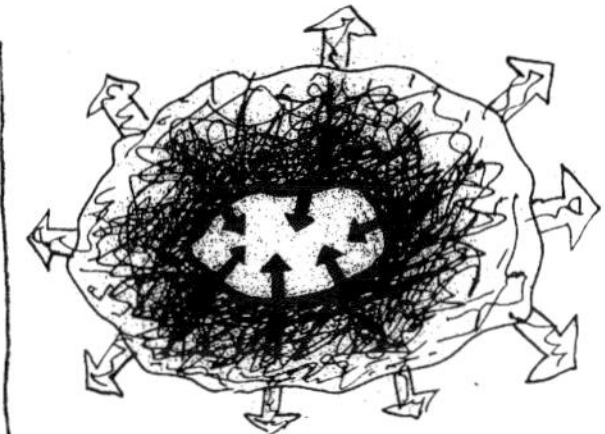

SUBURBS
FIRST
DESTROY the
LANDSCAPE & FORESTS
AND THEN
the
CITY

MOTORIZED ~ TRAFFIC

THE EFFECTS OF FUNCTIONAL ZONING

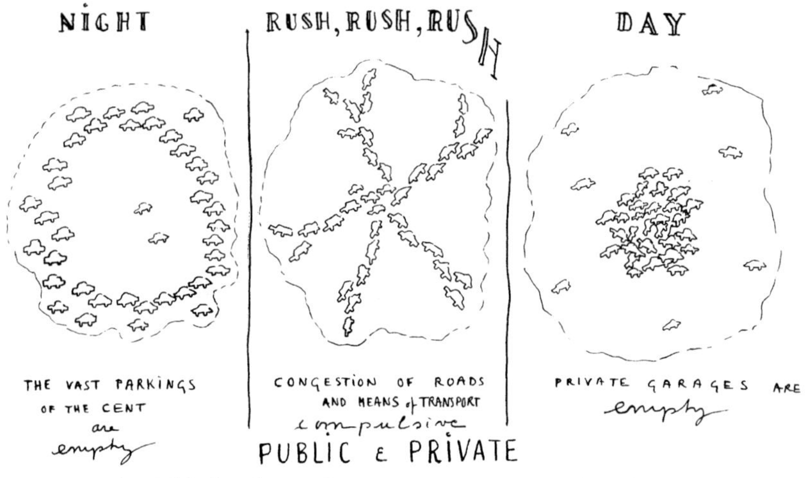

WASTAGE of human and chemical ENERGY

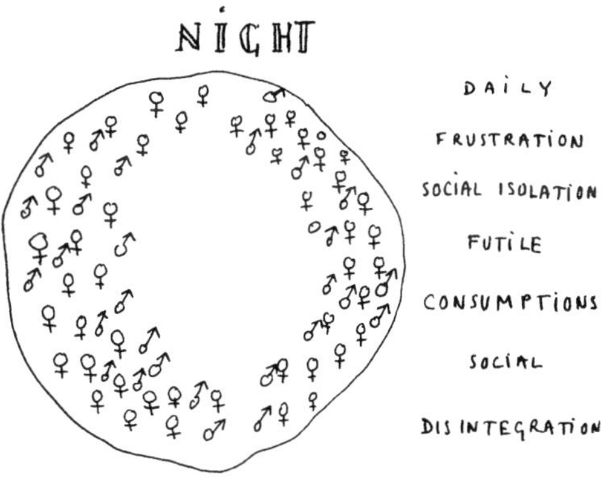
THE SEXES in the Anti-CITY
⇨ THE EFFECTS OF INDUSTRIALISATION
SOCIAL SEGREGATION of PLACES of PRODUCTION, AD-MINISTRATION ~ CONSUMPTION
NIGHT
DAY
DAILY
FRUSTRATION
SOCIAL ISOLATION
FUTILE
CONSUMPTIONS
SOCIAL
DISINTEGRATION
ALIENATION IN MINI-FAMILIES
DICTATORSHIP of MASS-MEDIAS
ALIENATION IN PLACES OF
PRODUCTION & ADMINISTRATION

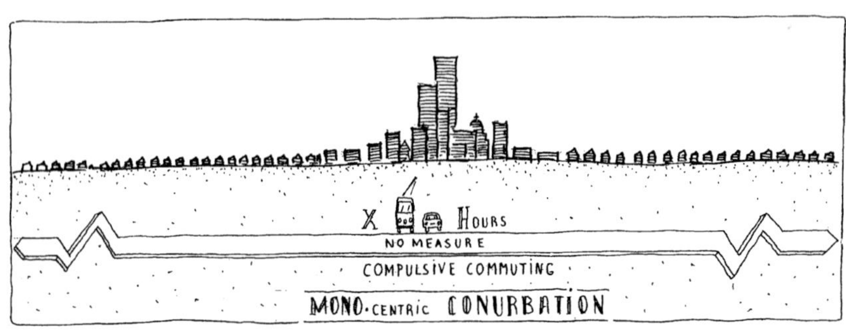
X HOURS
NO MEASURE
COMPULSIVE COMMUTING
MONO-CENTRIC CONURBATION

10 MINUTES
The STANDARD MEASURE
POLY-CENTRIC FEDERATION

NOT THE CAR BUT THE SUBURBAN HOME IS THE DEADLY WEAPON

DAILY SUBURBAN MORTARFIRE AGAINST URBAN CENTERS

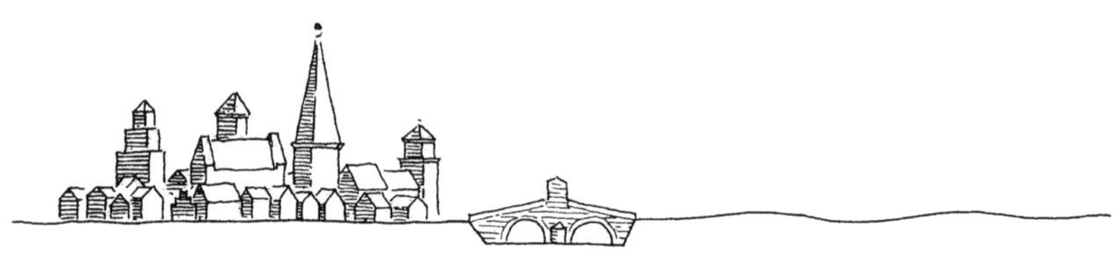

Mature CITY

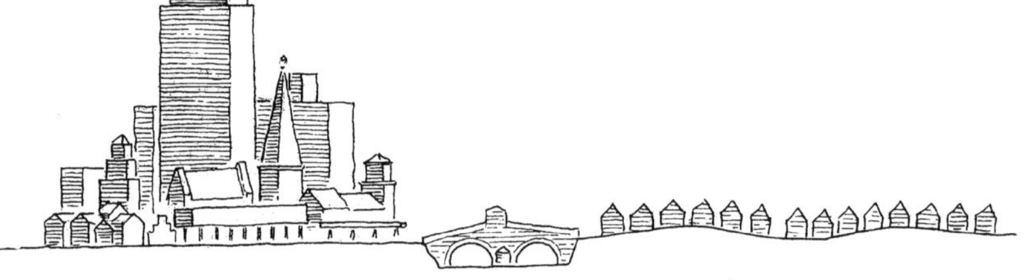

VERTICAL & HORIZONTAL "OVEREXPANSION"

Organic EXPANSION through DUPLICATION

1200
1500
1800
1900
2000
SLOW
ARCHITECTURE
FAST
ARCHITECTURE
accelerating
LK 80

COMPOSITION: ORGANIC VERSUS MECHANIC

Modes of Composition

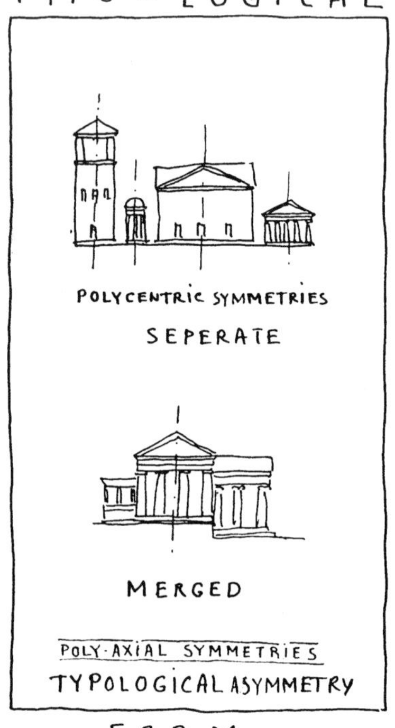

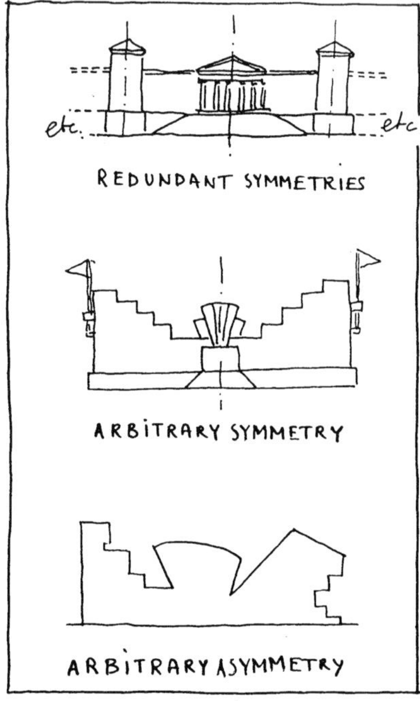

The MATERIAL of the COMPOSITION

The COMPLETE COMPOSITION

ORGANIC

The REDUNDANT SYMMETRIES

MECHANICAL

LK 84

I love her so, oh mother! classical

Iloveherso ohmother! vernacular

love
IIII lovehersososo ohmother
ohmother

academical, mechanical, capricious

l oooo

I ' eee

hh

rr

industrial (zoning)

False SYMMETRIES

CORRECT and FALSE SYMMETRIES

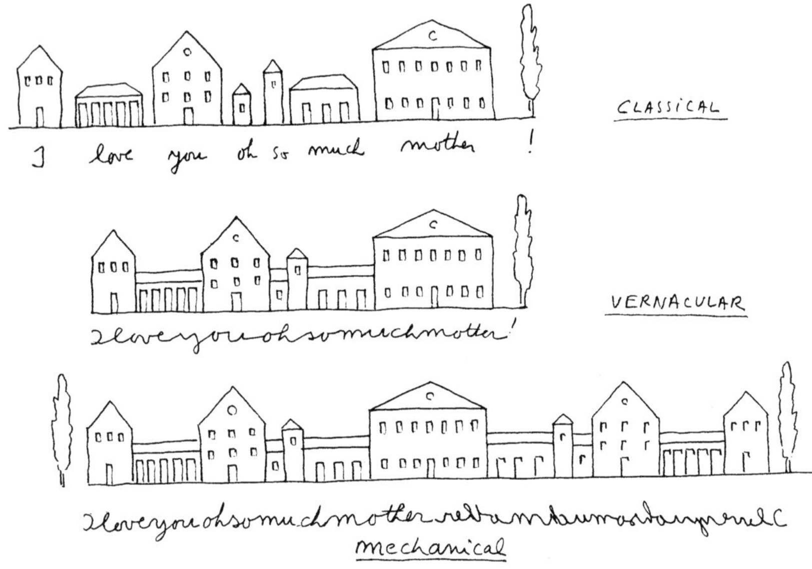

NATURAL SYMMETRY

NATURAL ARTISTIC ORDER

HIERARCHY

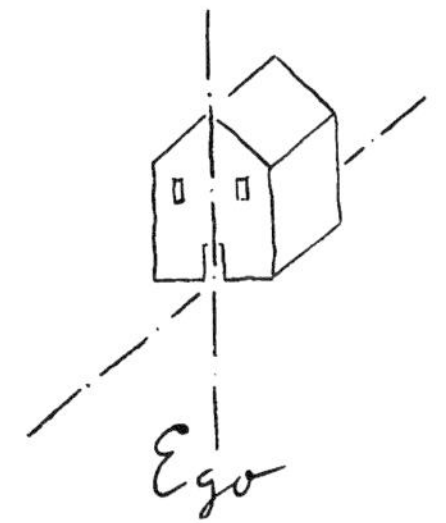

(UNIQUE) IDENTITY

INDIVIDUAL

Vernacular Crafts NATURE Classical Arts

Natural Hierarchy

of

Part and Whole

MECHANICAL SYMMETRY

TYRANNICAL ORDERING

A - HIERARCHICAL

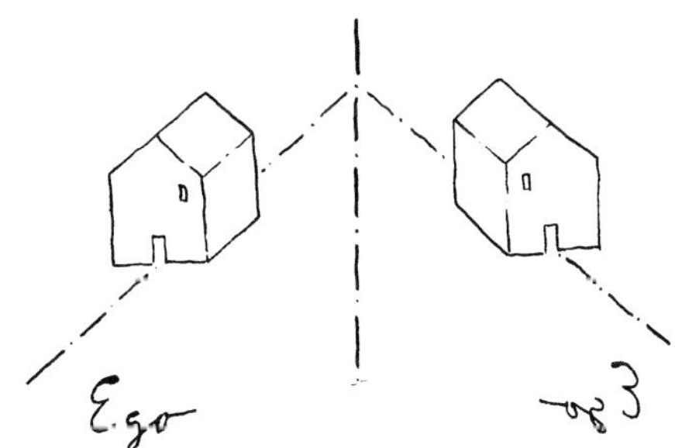

IDENTICAL IDENTITY

CLONE

Academic & Industrial

Tyrannical SUB-ordination

of

Part under Whole or Whole under Part

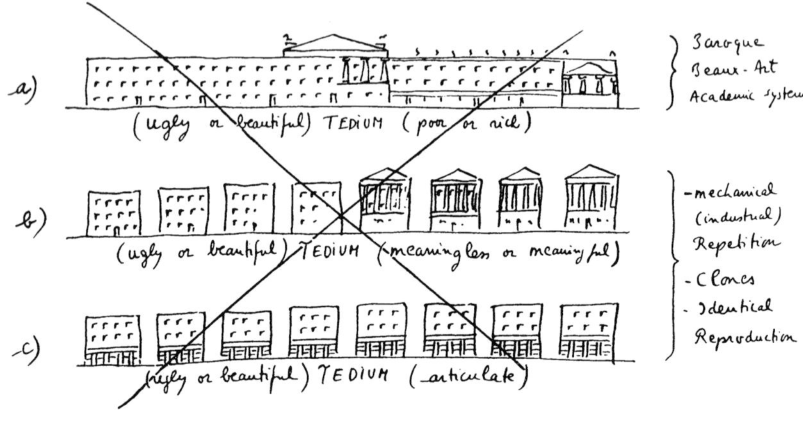
a)
(ugly or beautiful) TEDIUM (poor or rich)
Baroque
Beaux-Art
Academic system
b)
(ugly or beautiful) TEDIUM (meaningless or meaningful)
c)
(ugly or beautiful) TEDIUM (articulate)
-mechanical
(industrial)
Repetition
- Clones
- Identical
Reproduction

d)
(beautiful or ugly) City
Classical
Highest Form
Identity + Place

HIERARCHICAL COMPLEXITY CONTENT = FORM	ANTI-HIERARCHICAL COMPLEXITY	NON-HIERARCHICAL COMPLEXITY CONTENT X FORM
		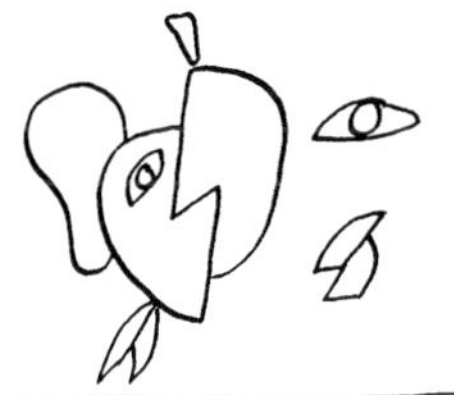

ORGANIC ORDER & SYMMETRY	MECHANICAL ORDER + SYMMETRY	PLANNED DIS-ORDER & COERCION
CLASSICAL	BAROQUE-ACADEMIC →	MODERNISMS, PUNK,
ORDER	ORDERING →	DECOMPOSTION as STYLE
RATIONALISM AS MEANS	RATIONALISM AS END	RATIONALISM as STYLE
INDIVIDUAL	CLONED →	INDIVIDUALISTIC {HIGH BROW / COMMERCIAL / TECHNO} KITSCH

TWO WORLDS

The two Worlds

The World
– as a solid, permanent
practical and beautiful
house (for) of mankind

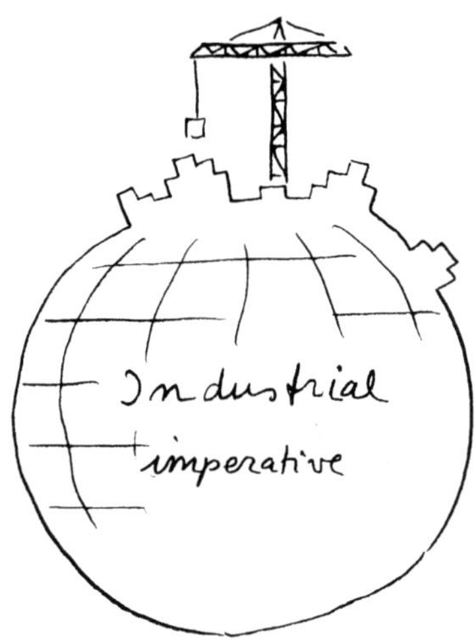

The Planet
– an endless, trivial
messy & noisy
building-site

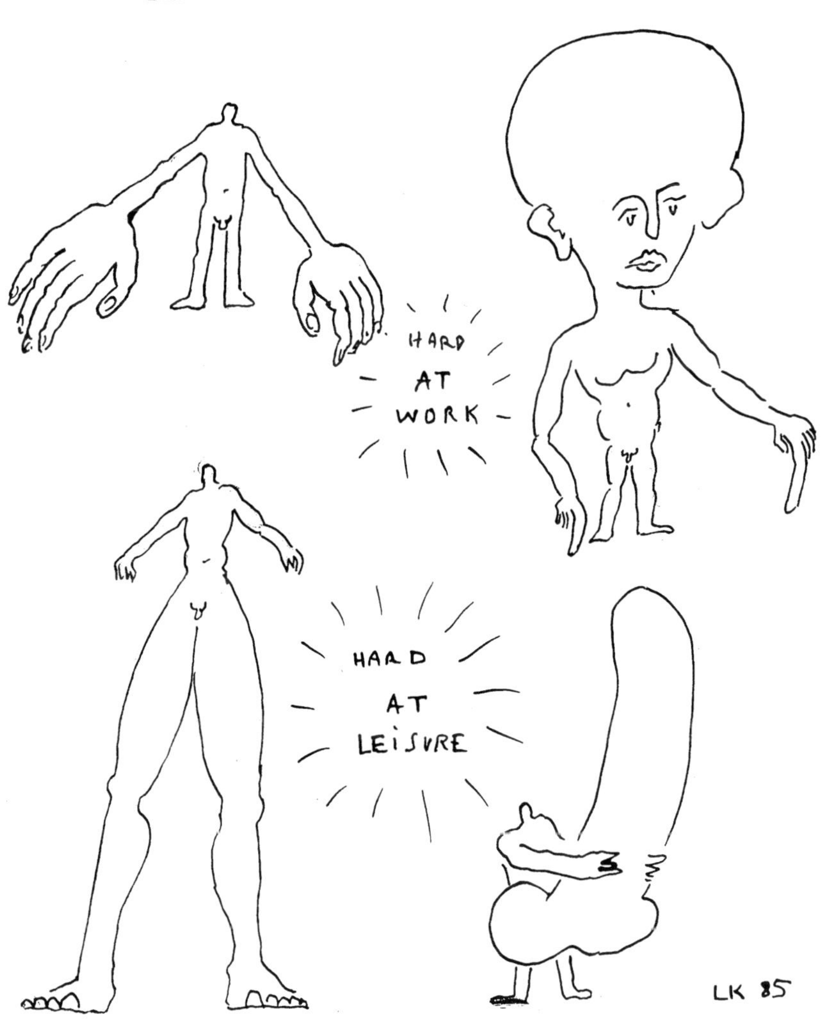
HOMO INDUSTRIALIS
HARD
AT
WORK
HARD
AT
LEISURE
LK 85

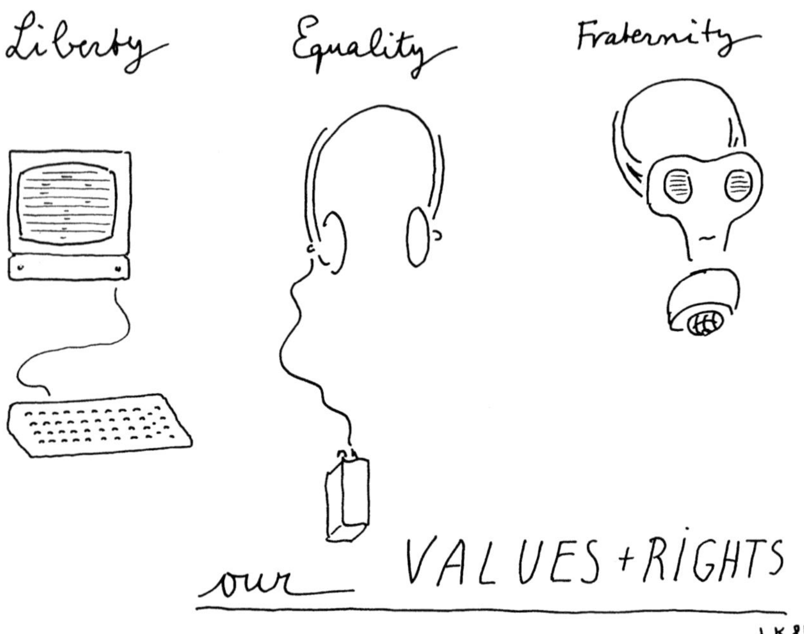
Liberty
Equality
Fraternity
our VALUES + RIGHTS
LK81

La vie industrielle

family stress

Work stress

age stress

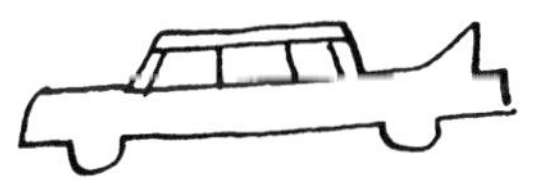

"I am at peace"

HIGH and LOW TECH

"THERE IS NO GOING BACK... dear"

(wishfull thinking)

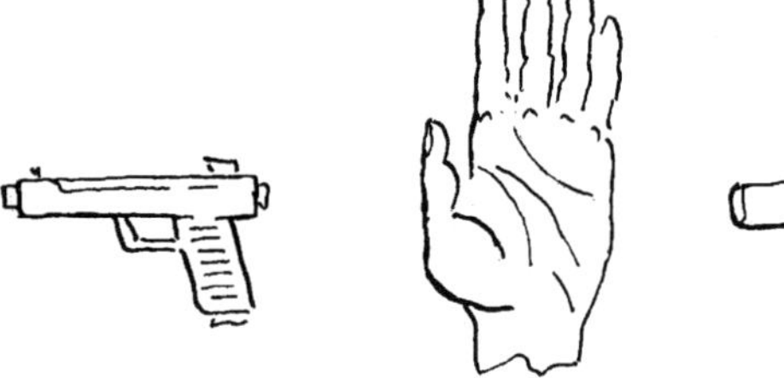

"MODERN" and "DATED"

FORMS OF HANDTOOLS

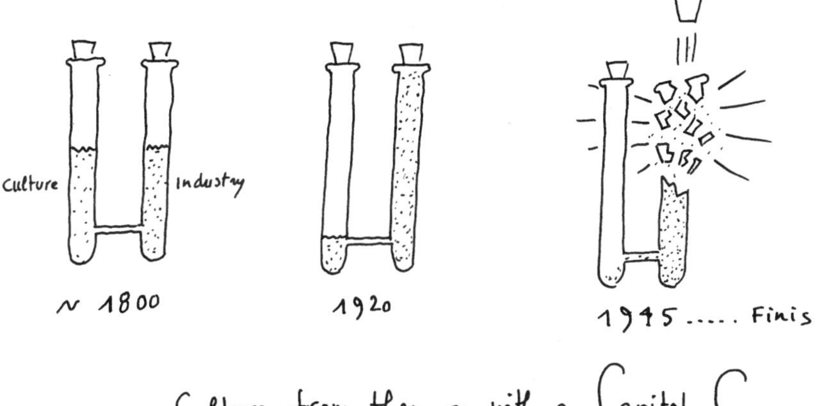
INDUSTRY ~ CULTURE
Culture
Industry
~ 1800
1920
1945 ..... Finis
Culture from then on with a Capital C...

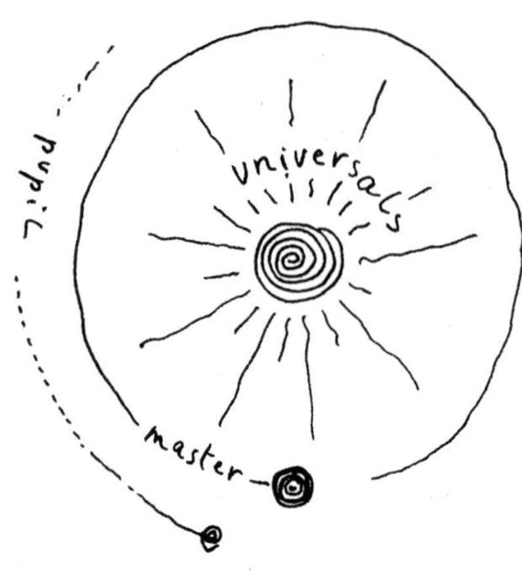

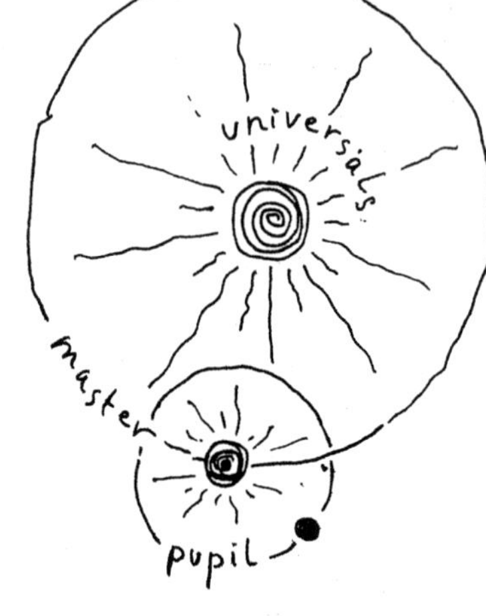

the good teacher

the bad teacher

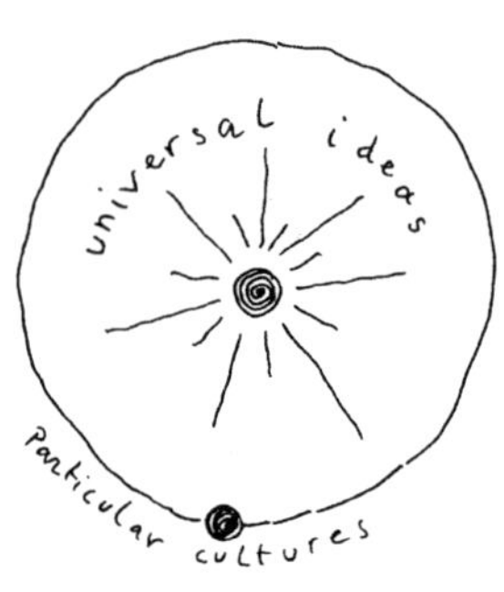

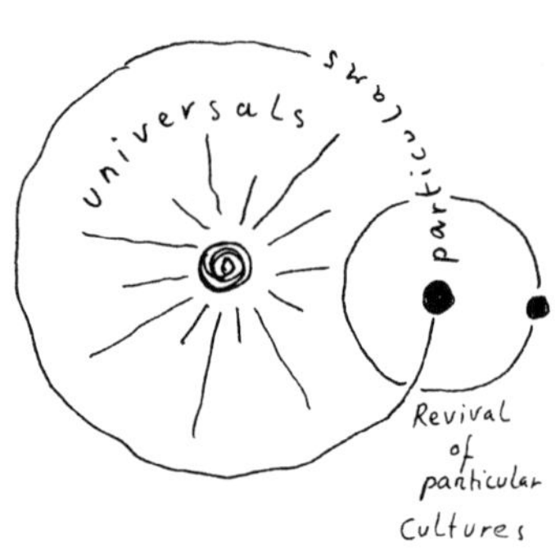

AUTHENTIC CULTURE

CULTURAL REVIVAL

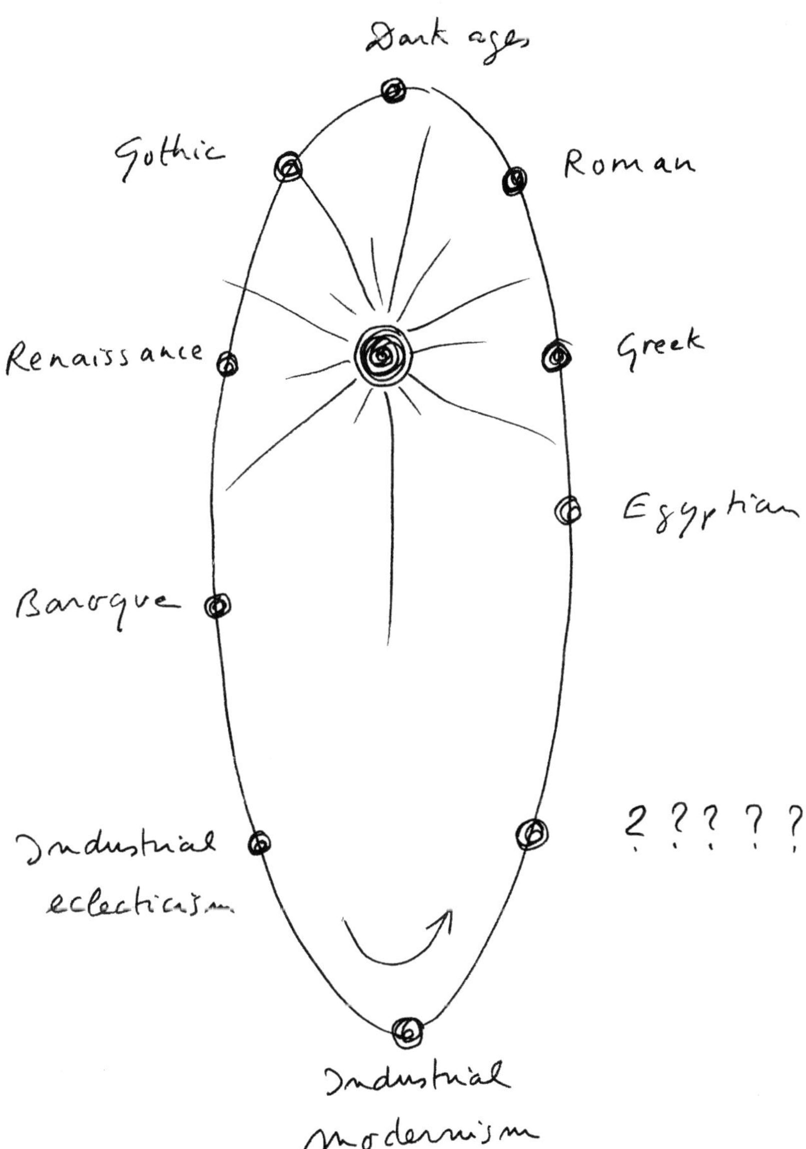
Dark ages
Gothic
Roman
Renaissance
Greek
Egyptian
Baroque
Industrial eclecticism
?????
Industrial modernism

l'architecte de l'ère machiniste

LEON KRIER · 16 BELSIZE PARK · LONDON N·W·3

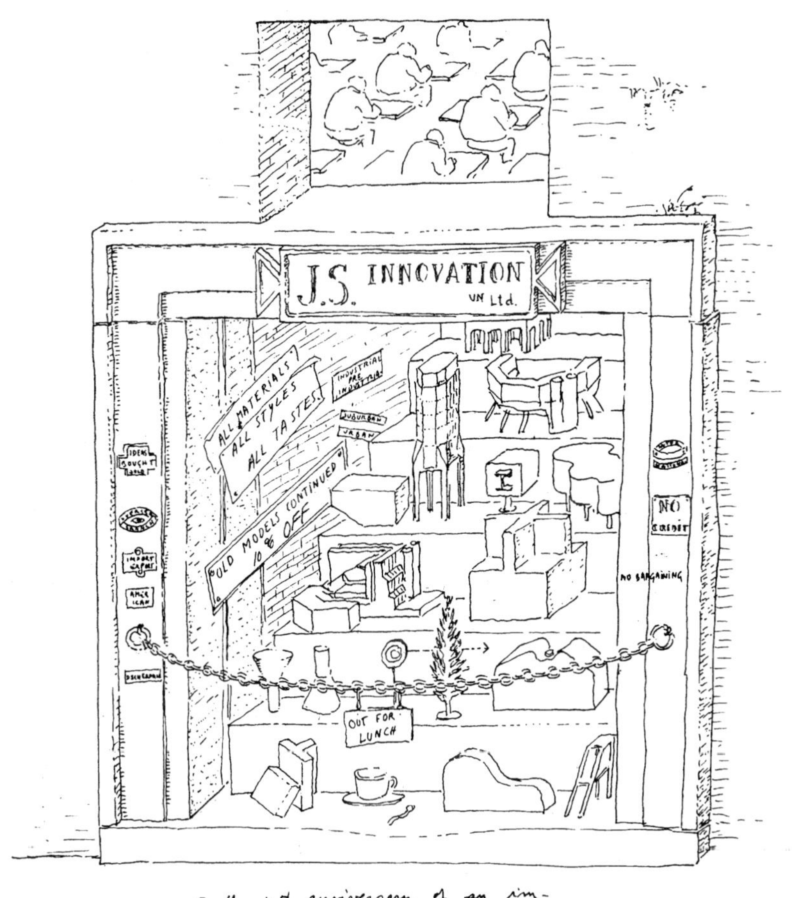

For the 10th anniversary of an im-
penetrable* relationship. best regards
MONDAY – 28 July 1968 – 1978 Léon 26/7/78

01 · 4358709

* probably immutable – and perfect

STYLES OF CONTEMPORARY
ARCHITECTURE COMMISSIONS
in
most "developed countries"

PUBLIC BUILDINGS

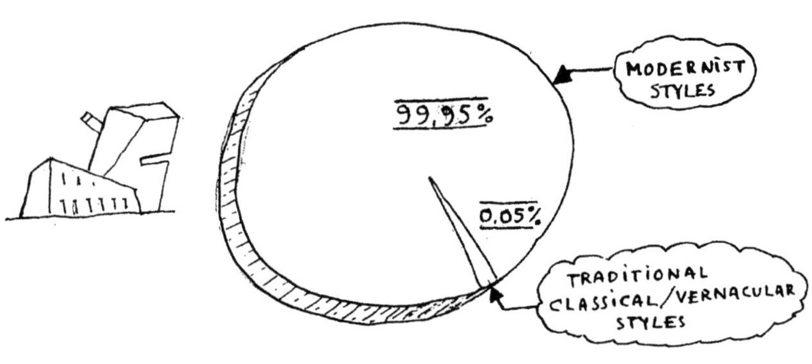

PRIVATE RESIDENTIAL

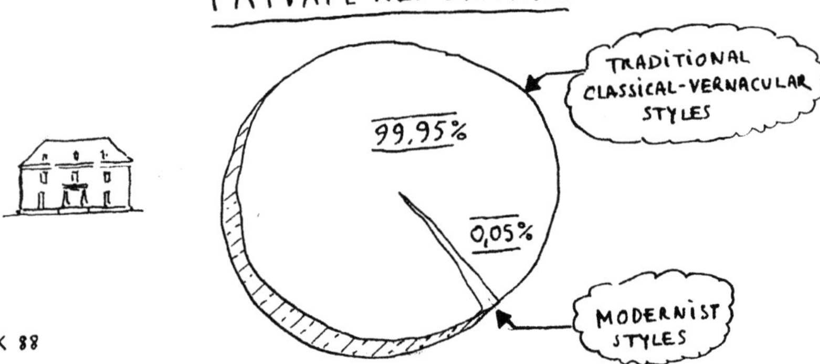

LK 88

ZEIT-TRIEB & ZEIT-GEIST

Industrial project and critical intellect

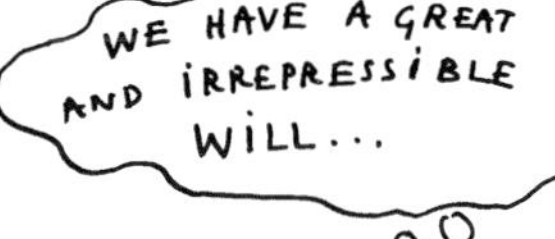

...and 150 years too late

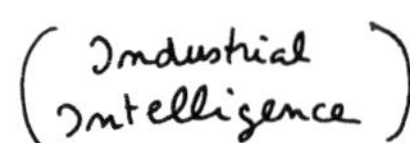

(Ecological
Intelligence)

LK81

The 2nd Greatest Achievement of ~~Industry~~ Collectivism

THE WILL TO DISCUSS, DECOMPOSE, CRITICIZE GROWS IN PROPORTION TO INCAPACITY of THINKING, COMPOSING, PROPOSING

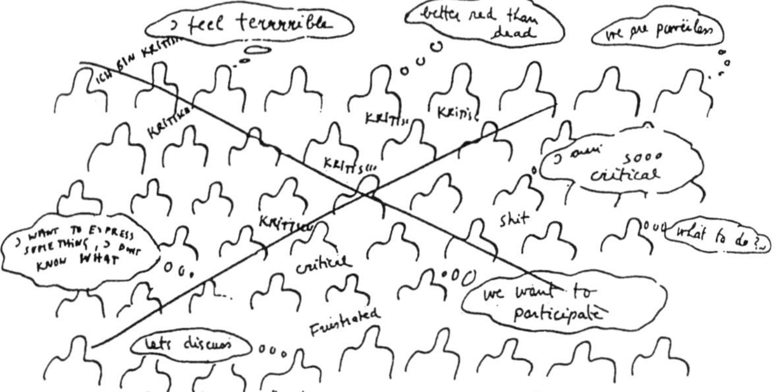

MILLIONS of INTELLIGENT BRAINS PERMANENTLY INCAPACITATED TO THINK AND WORK INDEPENDENTLY of INDUSTRIAL IDEOLOGY

The Greatest Achievement of ~~Industry~~ Collectivism

THE PRICE OF HANDWORK GROWS IN DIRECT DEPENDANCE WITH THE NUMBER of UNEMPLOYED HANDS

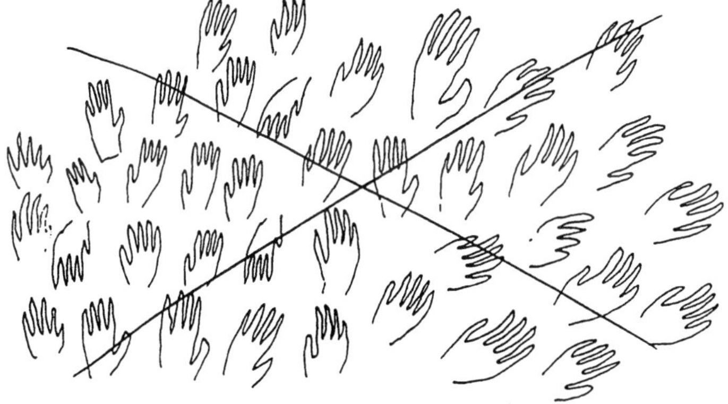

POTENTIAL COMPETITION TO INDUSTRIAL MONOPOLIES AND PRODUCTS EXCLUDED AND ELIMINATED PERMANENTLY THROUGH EDUCATED MASS-IGNORANCE AND MASS-UNEMPLOYMENT

THE REALM OF LIBERTY industrial-LEISURE-time LK81

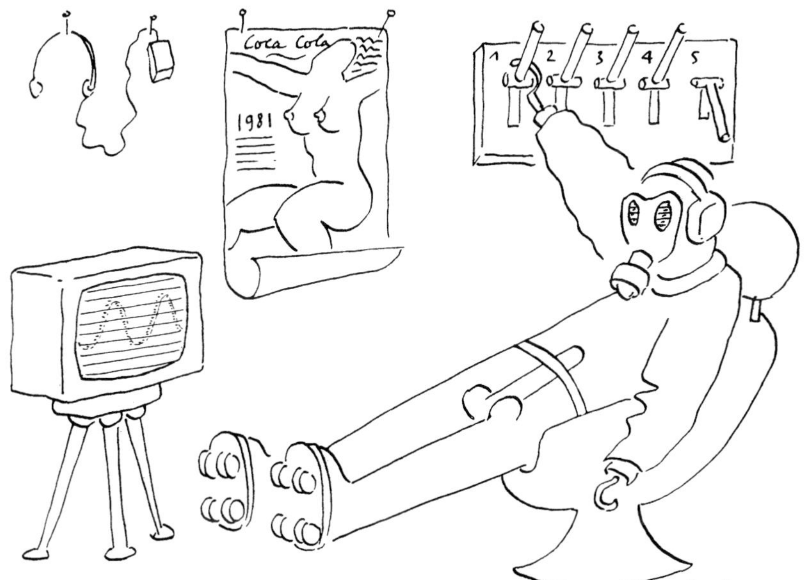

THE REALM OF NECESSITY industrial-TOILING-time LK81

False PLURALISM
• NO POSSIBILITY OF CHOICE •

True PLURALITY
• FREEDOM OF CHOICE •

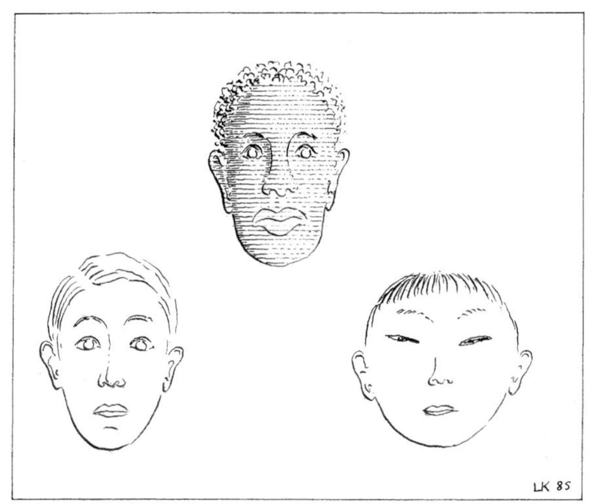

Traditional Pluralism

modernist Pluralism

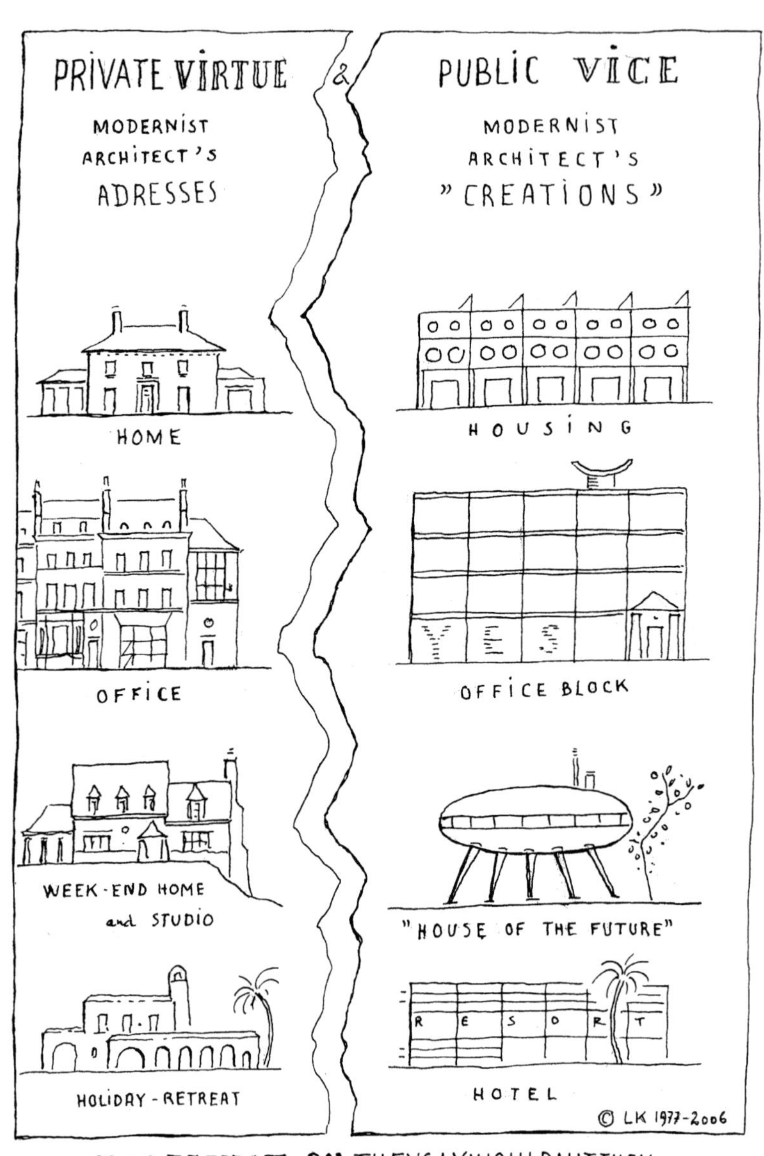

"SO WHAT ?" THEYSAY,WOULDN'TTHEY:

REAL ESTATE Agency
SCHOOL OF ARCHITECTURE
PROF. ALPHA
PROF. BETA
PROF. DELTA
PROF. GAMMA
LK84

"SPIRIT OF TIME" WINNING AGAINST "SPIRIT OF PLACE"
("Cutting-edge" spirit being a child of cosy environment)

how cynical!
how uncompromising!
LK
88
CONTEMPORARY INSIDE~OUTSIDE DESIGN ROUTINE

MODERN Traditional

MODERN Traditional & Modernist

MODERN Modernist

BEAUBOURG ?

LK 93

BEAUBOURG !

ACTUAL + SYMBOLIC

VALUES

natural - artificial

TRUE

SYMBOLIC

VALUE

SOCIAL CONVENTION

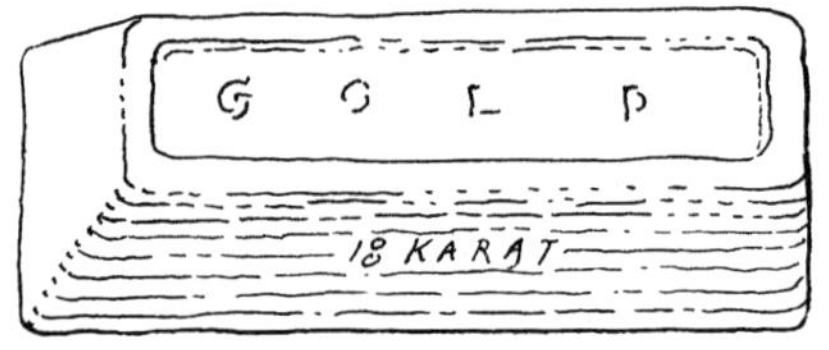

TRUE

NATURAL

VALUE

CHEMICAL FACT

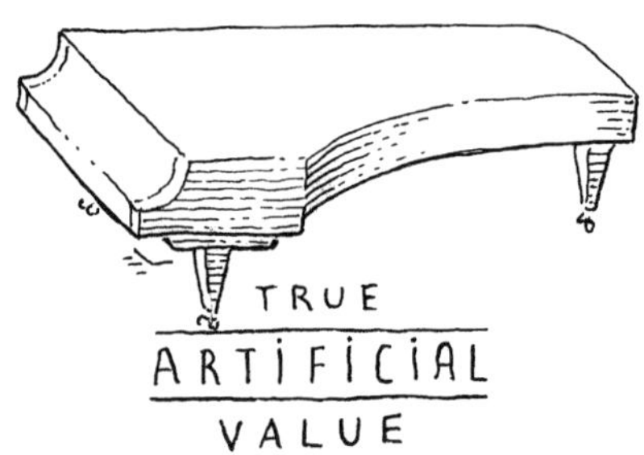

TRUE

ARTIFICIAL

VALUE

PHYSICAL FACT

LK 03

Two Forms of Accumulation

Could this be
a
wine bottle?
Could this be
a
Coffee Pot?
wine
Coffee

ARCHITECTURE
(WITH SCULPTURE)

SCULPTURE

PAINTING

L.K. 88

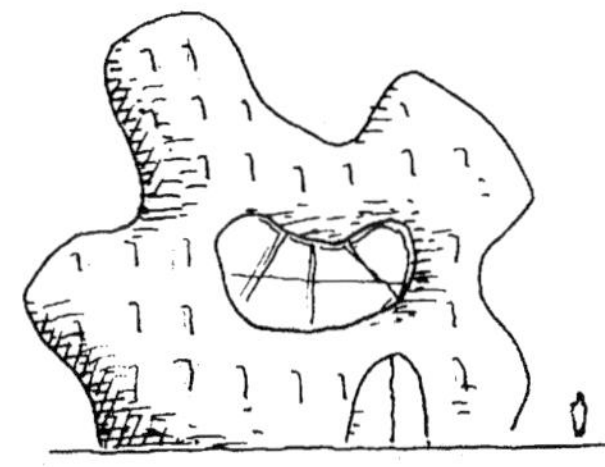
SO~CALLED
ARCHITECTURE

SO~CALLED
SCULPTURE

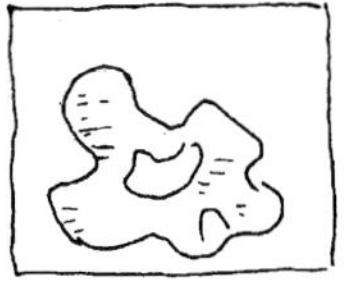
SO~CALLED
PAINTING

THERE IS NO GOiNG... ERR...
GROWING BACK... CHiLD
WHEN I AM BIG
I WANT TO GROW
SMALL LiKE iM
DADDY.........

COMFORT ~ MODEL and
good measure
traditions
made to measure
INTELLIGENT CONVENTION

modernisms
"CREATIVE"
SCHIZZO ~ PARANOÏAC CONVENTION
LK 83

MIES · CENTENNIAL · PROPOSAL

FUTURE OF MÏES ~ ANTHROPY

MORE MIES IS LESS

MIES PRIVATE FURNISHINGS PROMINENTLY DISPLAYED IN "MIESLAND"-SHRINE

BLODDY CONFOORMIST
LK 85

Architects against Boredom
we demand bla bla
Architects
against
ARCHITECTS FOR SOCIAL Responsabitity
Architects FOR MINORITIES
ARCHITECTS FOR Peace
ARCHITECTS For ARCHITECTURE
WOAWWW

LK86
YOU CANNOT TURN BACK THE WHEEL... YOU CAN'T GO BACK ...YOUNG MAN...
TALK FOR YOURSELF... OLD MAN...

MODERN HYDRA

LK 1984

THE URBAN MAN

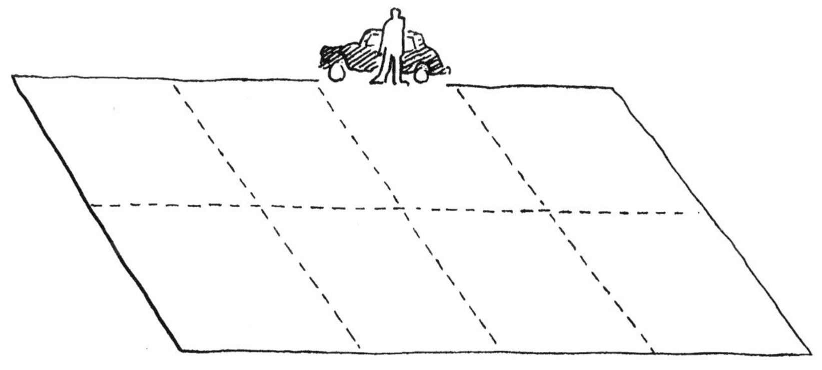

THE SUB-URBAN MAN

MAN · VEHICLE · LANDNEED

FROM SMALL TO LARGE FAMILY (I)

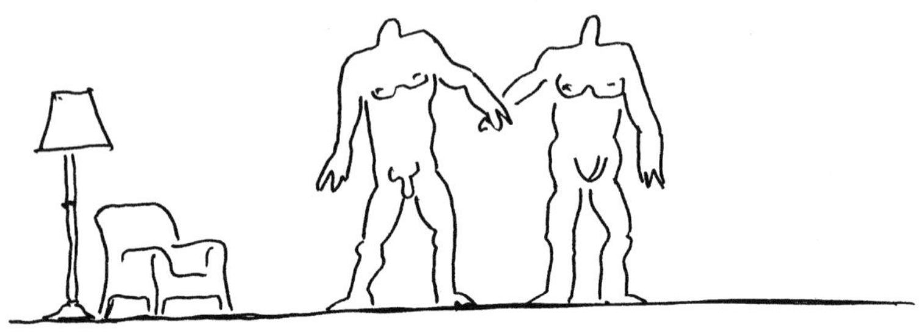

ORGANIC FORM OF GROWTH

MULTIPLICATION

FROM SMALL TO LARGE FAMILY (II)

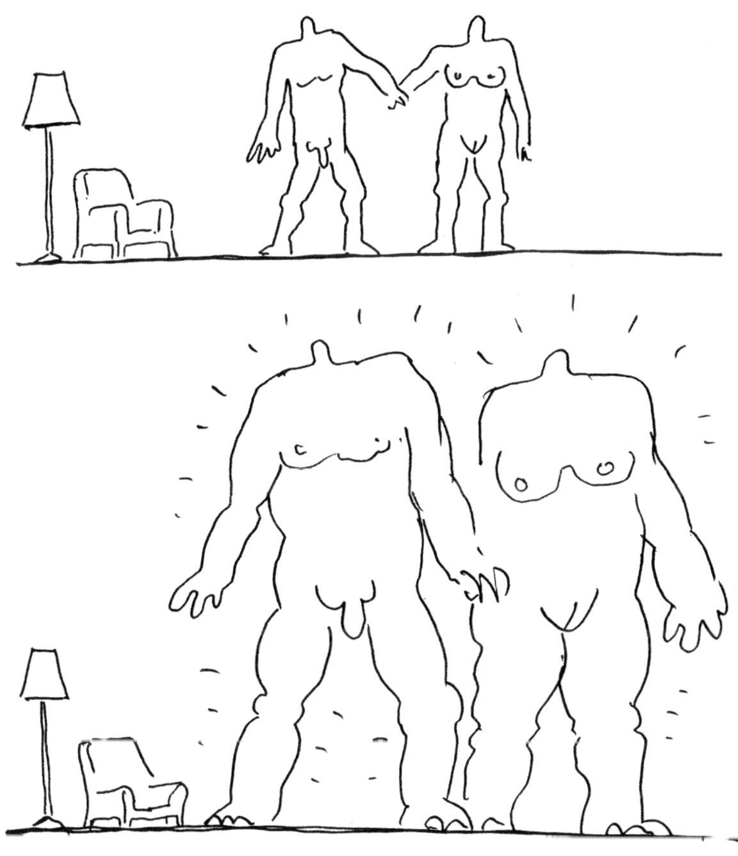

MONSTROUS FORM OF GROWTH

OBESITY

CORRECT URBAN GROWTH

IMMATURE QUARTERS GROW TILL MATURITY

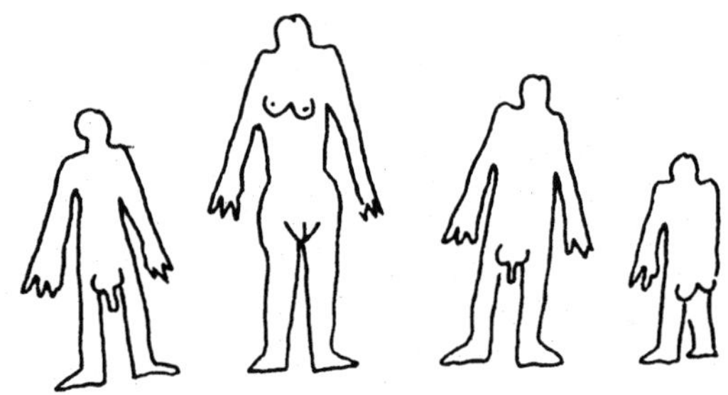

CATASTROPHIC ANTI-URBAN GROWTH

MATURE PARTS DEGRADE INTO FRAGMENTS

Urban GROWTH

ORGANIC versus MECHANIC

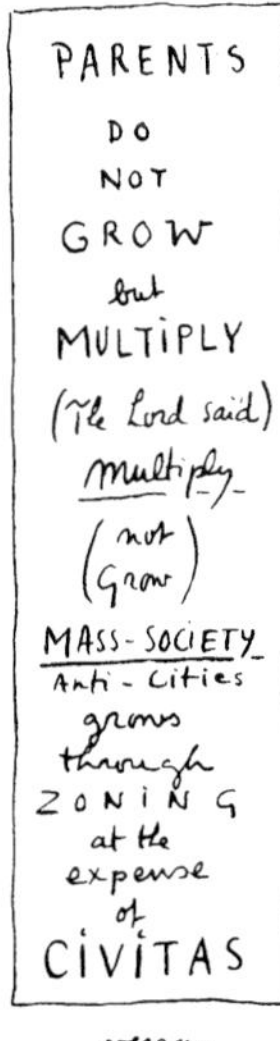

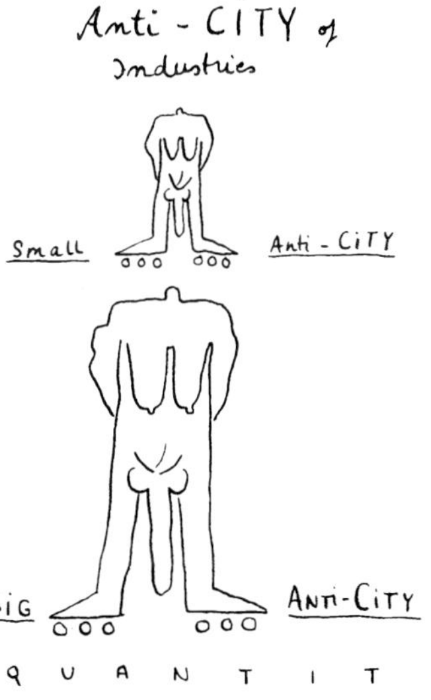

The Columbus Factor

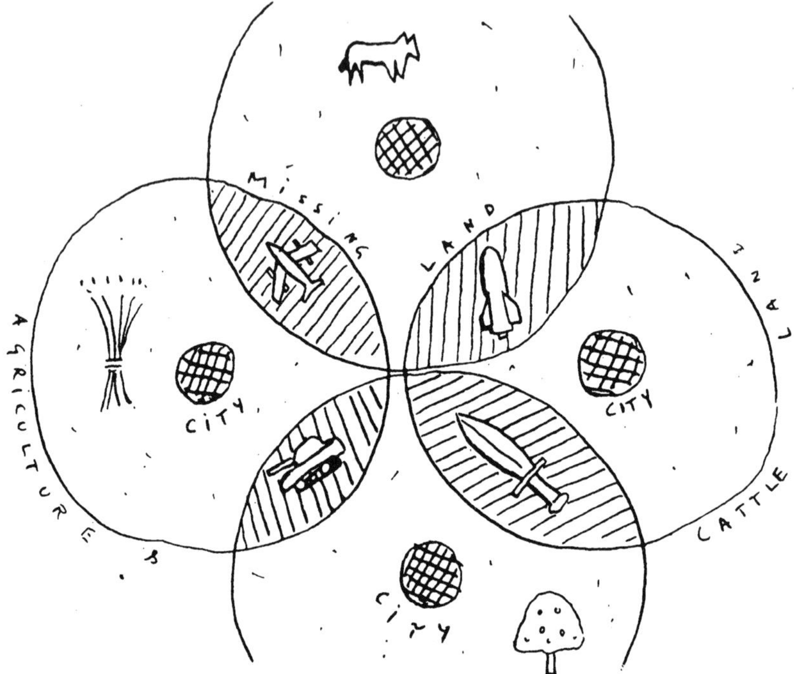

X Number of Cities need X times more Land

For whatever Land they are missing they are going to bash in their own heads and rather than reduce their own numbers, they are going to invade, conquer and subjugate far Lands, continents and peoples

City
&
LANDSCAPE

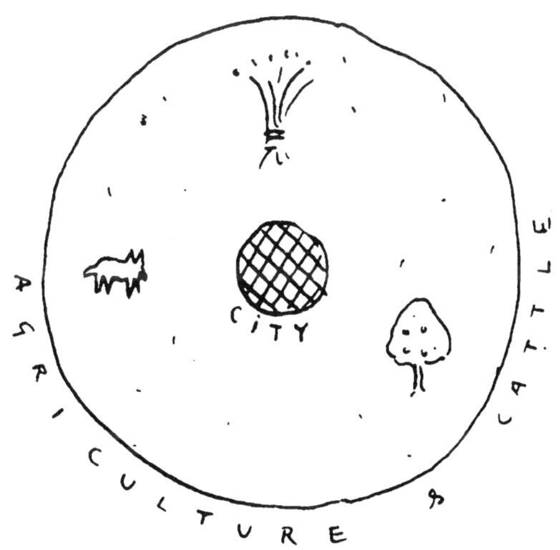

A CITY needs APPROX
so much land
for its nutrition

LK 1982

50'000 OCCUPANTS OF WORLD TRADE CENTER

VOLUME OF FUEL CONSUMPTION

IN 31 MONTHS AT RATE OF 2006

(7 BILLION BARRELS PER YEAR FOR 230'000'000 CITIZENS)

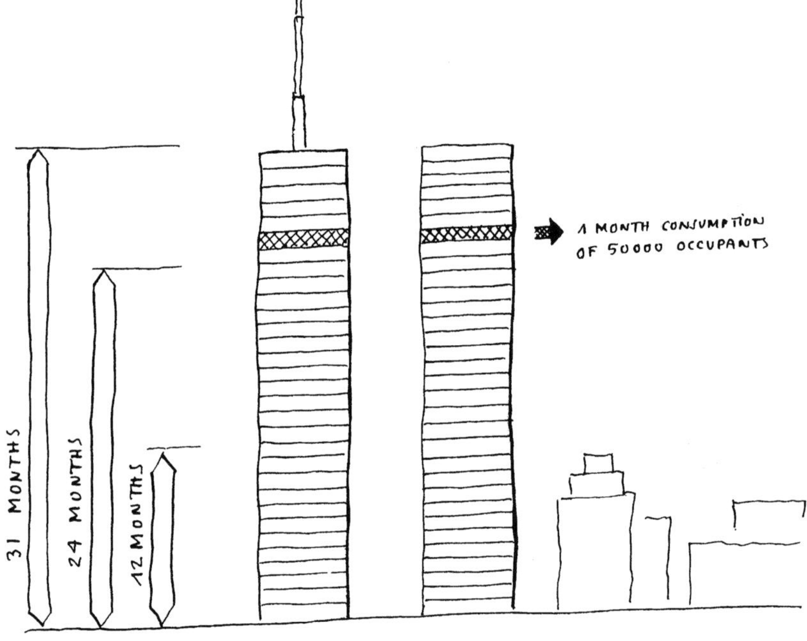

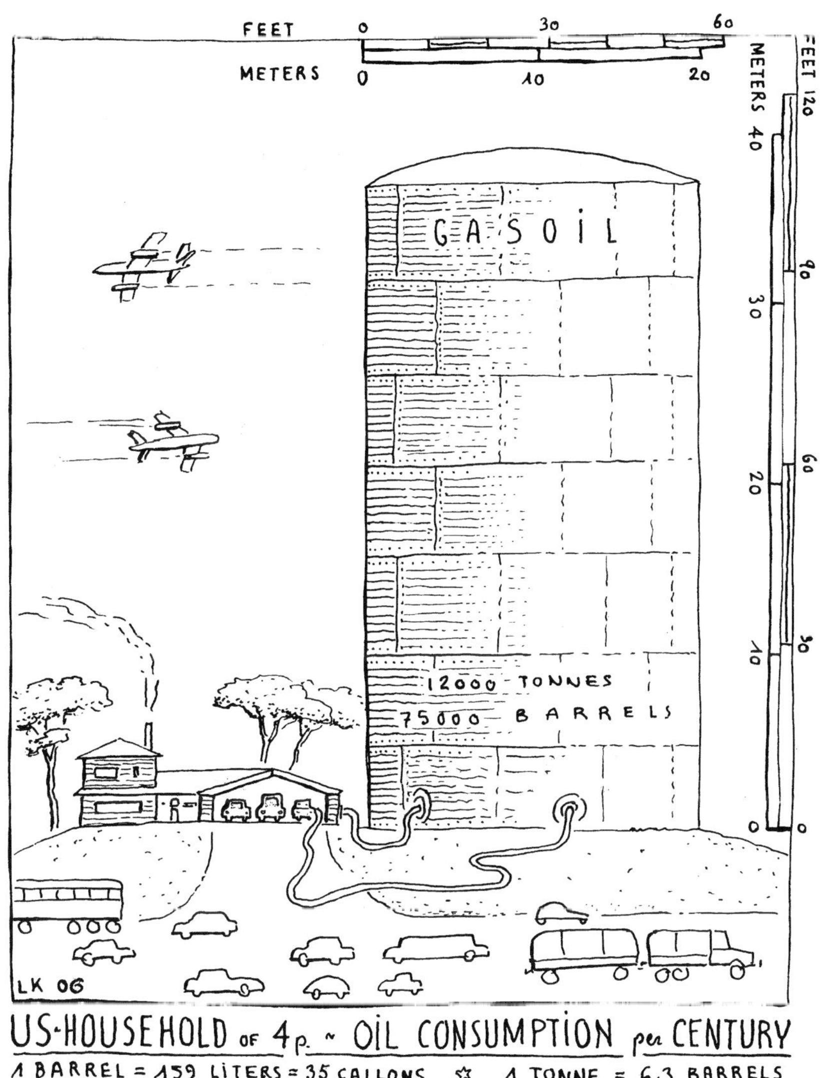
FEET 0 30 60
METERS 0 10 20
METERS 40 30 20 10 0
FEET 120 90 60 30 0
GASOIL
12000 TONNES
75000 BARRELS
LK 06
US-HOUSEHOLD of 4p. ~ OIL CONSUMPTION per CENTURY
1 BARREL = 159 LITERS = 35 GALLONS ☆ 1 TONNE = 6.3 BARRELS

GLOBAL WARMING

WHAT CAUSES

BRAIN WARMING

AND LET ME TELL THE AMERICAN CITIZENS ONE THING.... WE ARE PREPARED TO DO ANYTHING IN ORDER TO SAVE ENGERGY; BUT I CAN ASSURE YOU ALL OF ONE THING,... WE AMERICANS WILL NEVER GIVE UP OUR AMERICAN WAY OF LIFE

A. SCHLESINGER - WORLD ENERGY CONFERENCE WASHINGTON 1977

LK 78

BRAIN power S
(LIMITED)

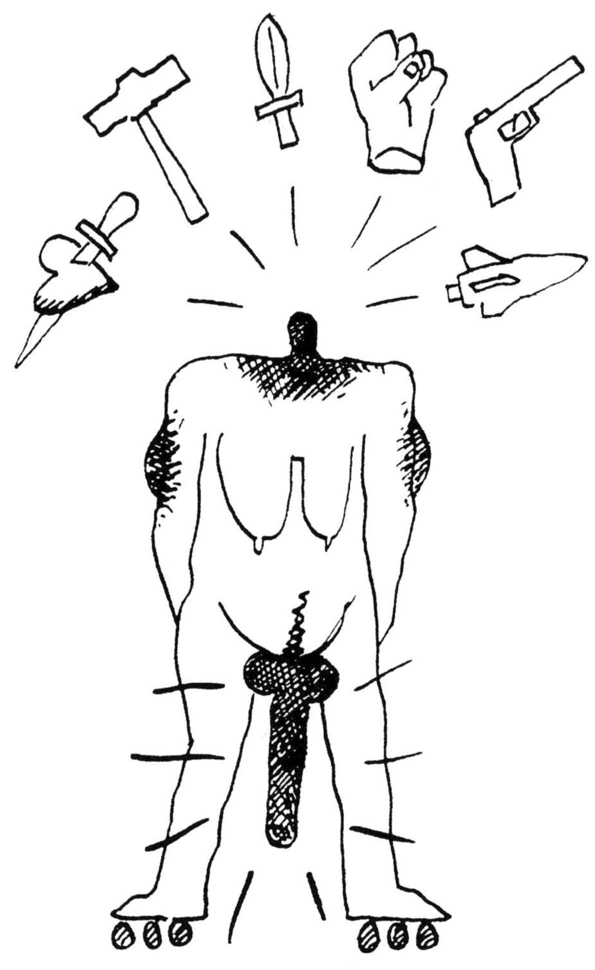

HOMO INDUSTRIALIS

HOMO FABER

MIMICRY

creative or slavish

I love

model
(message)

I love

I love
I LOVE
I love
I LOVE
I love
I love
I LOVE
I LOVE

IMITATION

I love
I lure
I luri
I live
Iliri
Iliri

SEMANTIC MIMICRY

sane
creative
sense producing

LK 07

GRAPHIC MIMICRY

insane
slavish
non-sense producing

BUILDINGS AND URBAN SPACES

THE FOUR FUNDAMENTAL TYPES OF URBAN SPACE

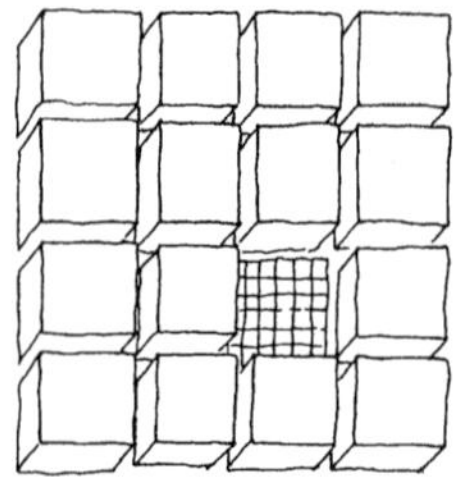

The Blocks are the result of a street and square pattern...

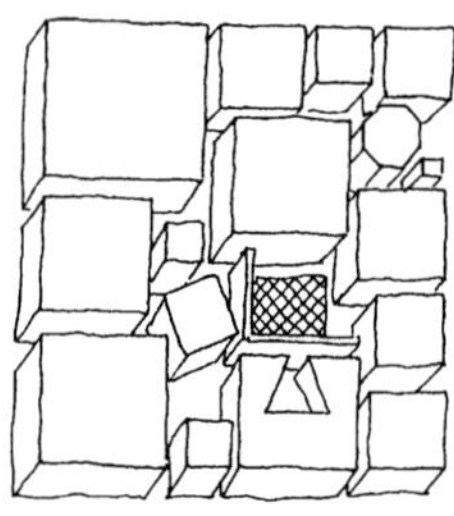

The streets and squares are the result of the position of the blocks...

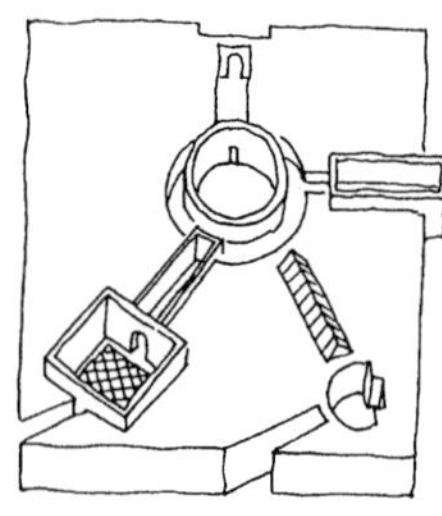

The streets and squares are precise formal types,

the block is a result

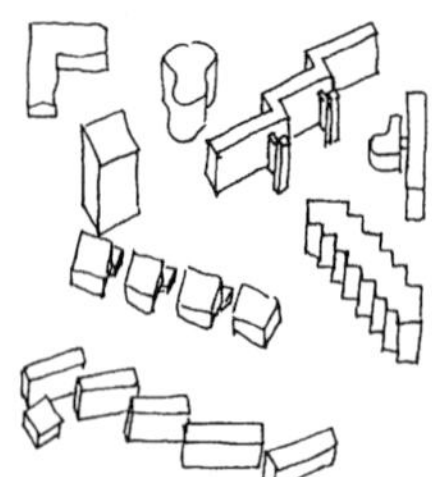

The objects do not form a describable space,

the public space is an accidental left-over

LK 77

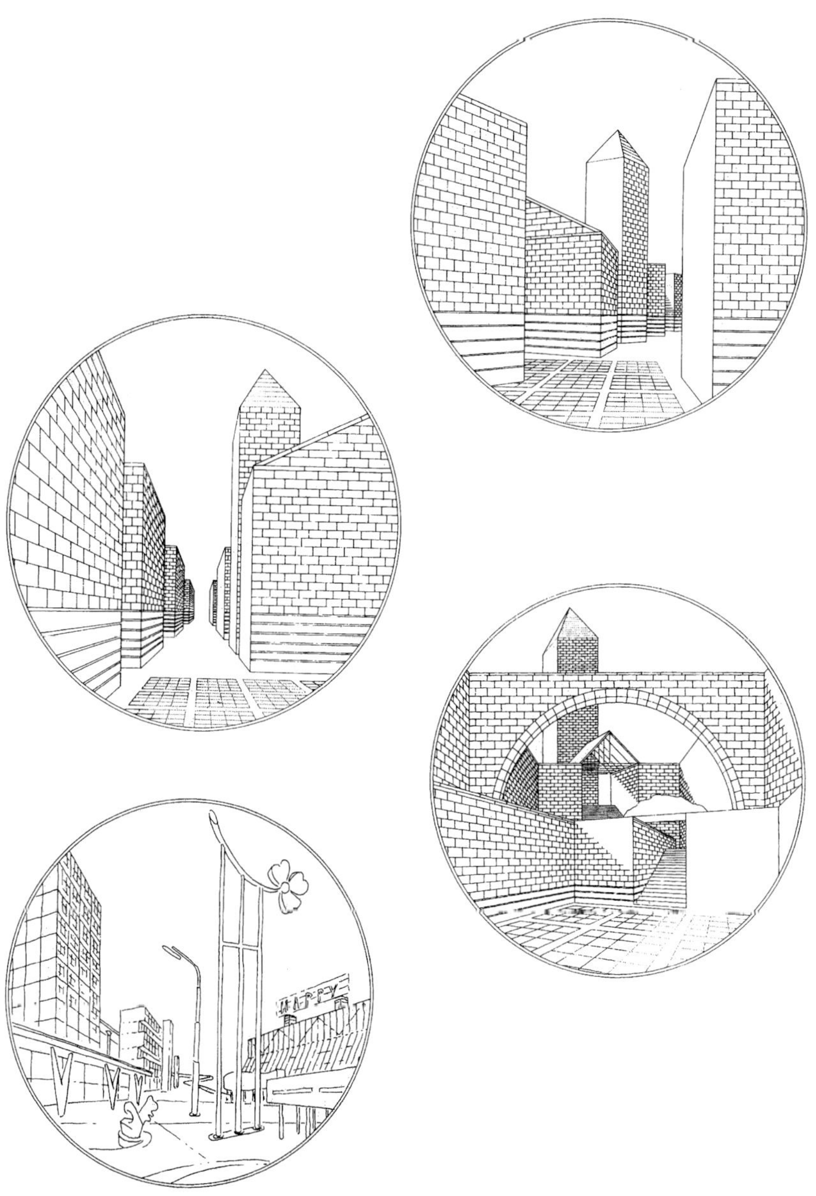
HAPPY

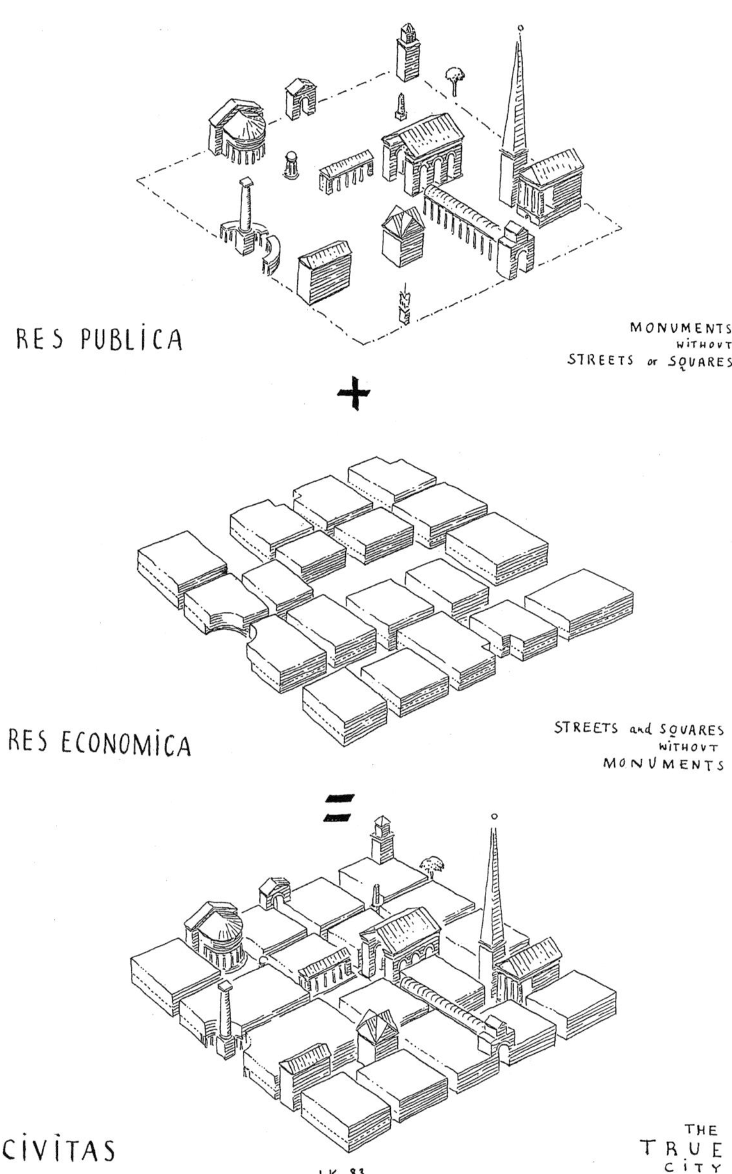
RES PUBLICA
MONUMENTS
WITHOUT
STREETS or SQUARES
+
RES ECONOMICA
STREETS and SQUARES
WITHOUT
MONUMENTS
=
CIVITAS
LK 83
THE
TRUE
CITY

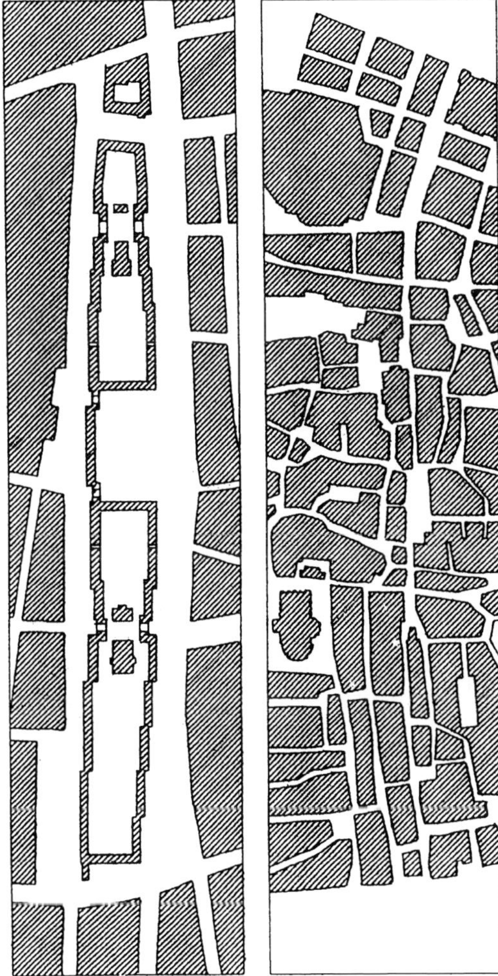
VIENNA
KARL-MARX HOF
HISTORICAL CENTER
3 ARCHITECTS
~ 3 HA ~
345 ARCHITECTS
~ 3 HA ~
5,1 KM • PUBLIC FRONTAGE • 18.5 KM

RELATIVE QUANTITY

1850 ~ 1920

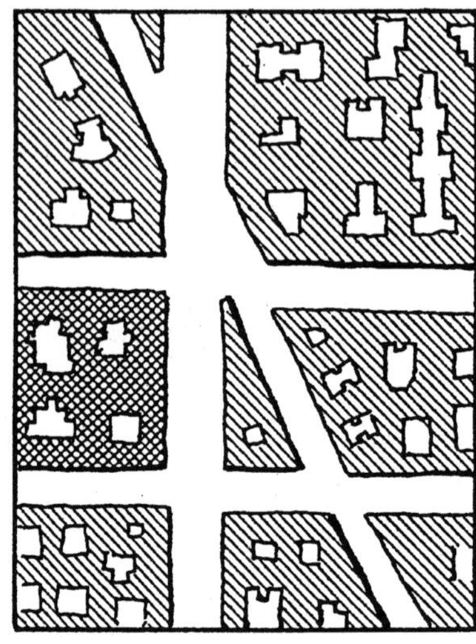

15 ~ 20 %

TOO LITTLE PUBLIC SPACE

1945 ~ 1968

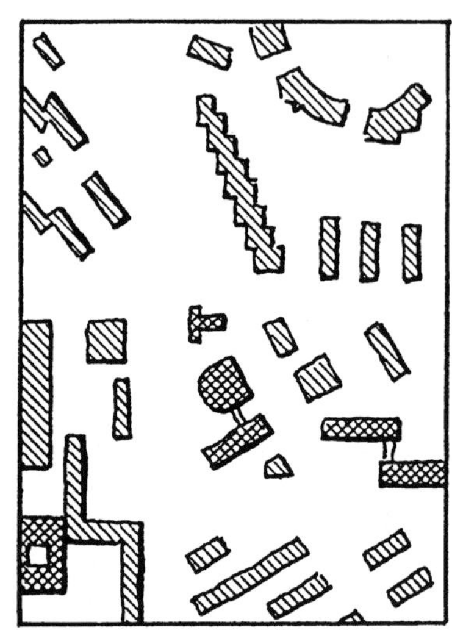

70 ~ 80 %

TOO MUCH PUBLIC SPACE

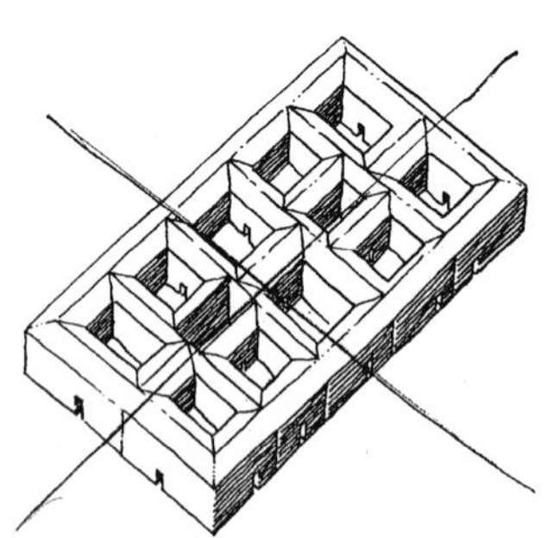

15 – 20 % of public space

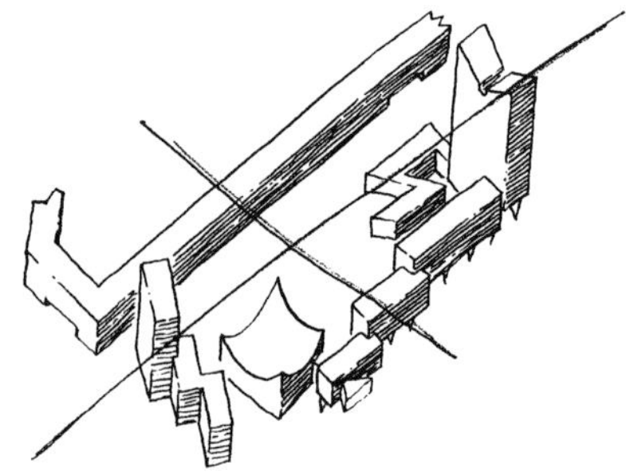

70 – 80 % of public space

of PUBLIC SPACE

1970 ~ 1980

OPTIMUM

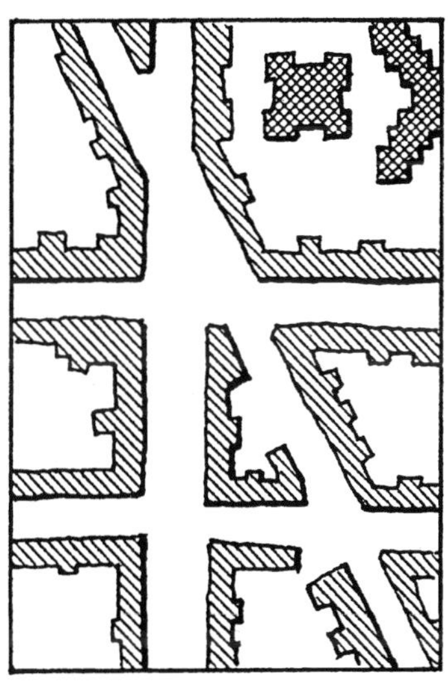

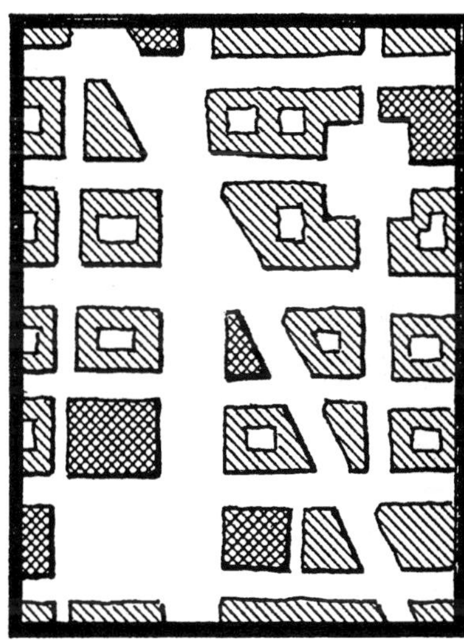

50 ~ 60 %
TOO MUCH SEMI-PUBLIC

25 ~ 35 %
THE GOOD PROPORTION

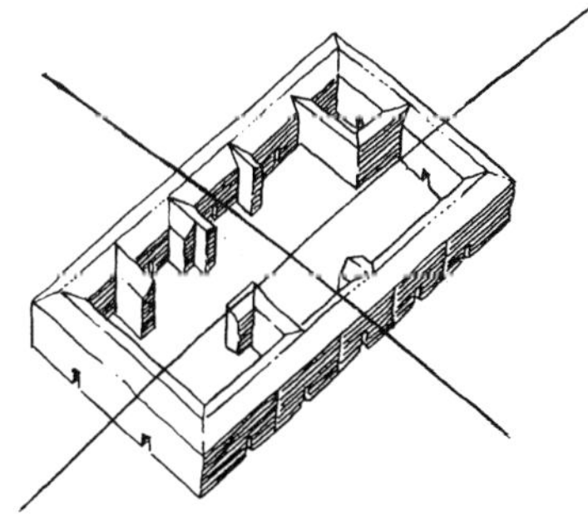

50 – 60 % of public space

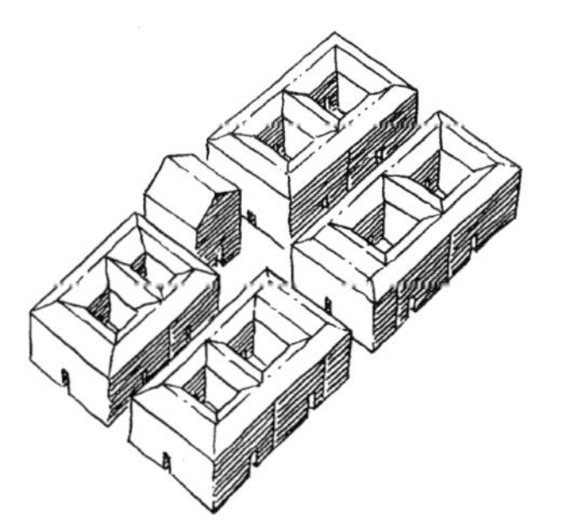

25 – 35 % of public space

NOT the BERLIN - BLOCK was WRONG but its MEASURES were WRONG
NOT the appartment to the STREET was wrong, the one into the COURT was WRONG
NOT the LENGTH of the STREET is a PROBLEM, the LENGTH of the BLOCK is the PROBLEM

car-traffic remains in the existing street
– pedestrian streets and squares inside the new Blocks –

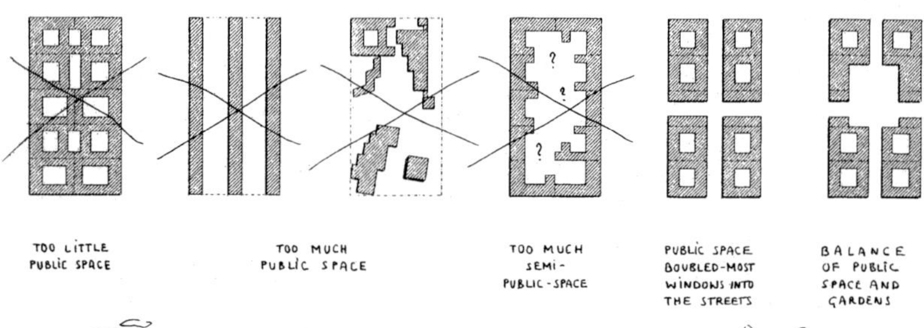

no police

NO DAY-LIGHT -WAIST OF PUBLIC MONEY - VANDALISM - BOREDUM - - LITTLE PUBLIC COST - SOCIAL COHESION

LK77

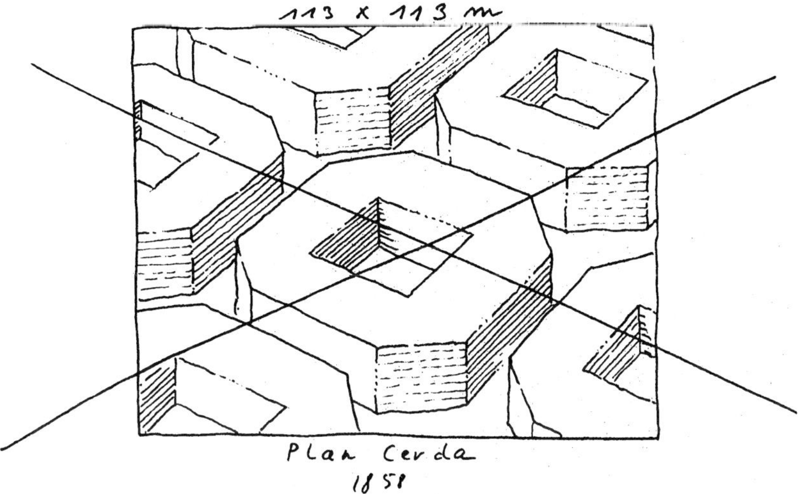
113 x 113 m
Plan Cerda
1858

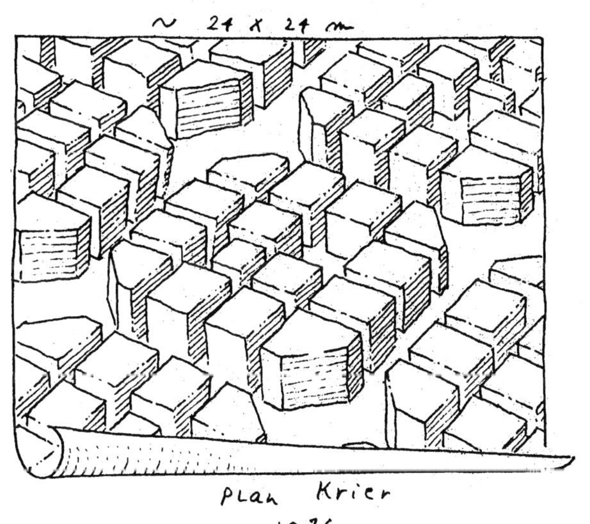
~ 24 x 24 m
plan Krier
1976

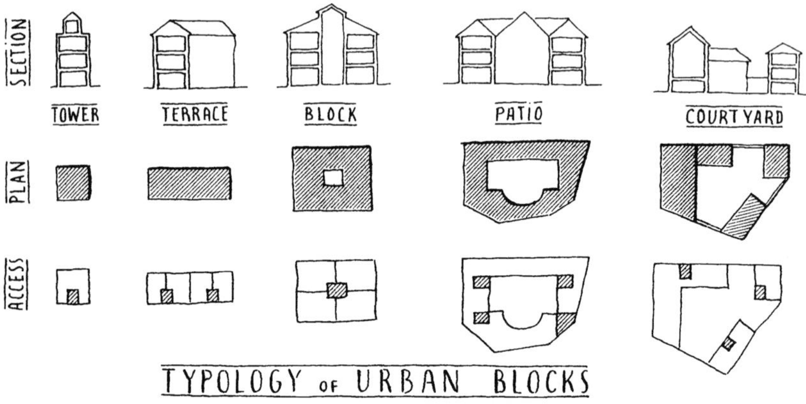
SECTION
TOWER
TERRACE
BLOCK
PATIO
COURTYARD
PLAN
ACCESS
TYPOLOGY OF URBAN BLOCKS

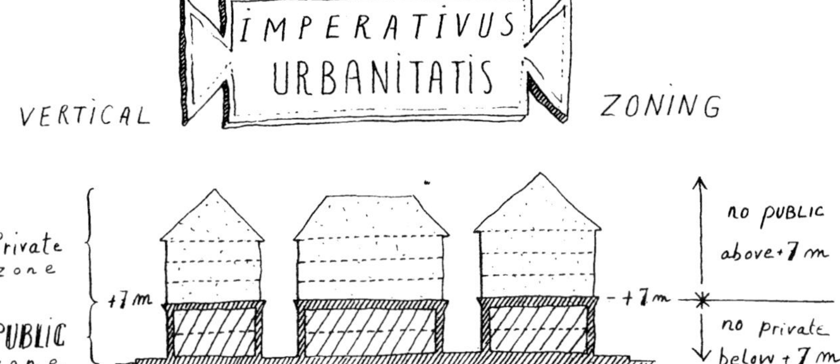

VERTICAL zoning versus HORIZONTAL zoning

The only NECESSARY and SUFFICIENT form of ZONING

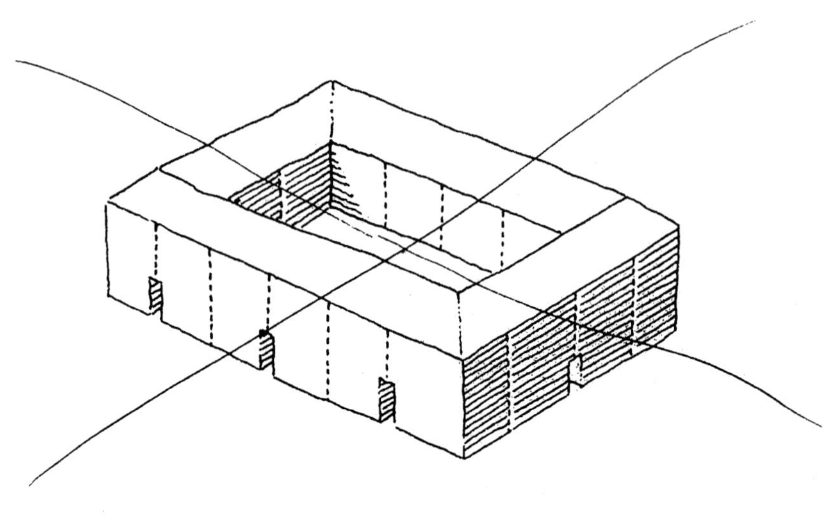

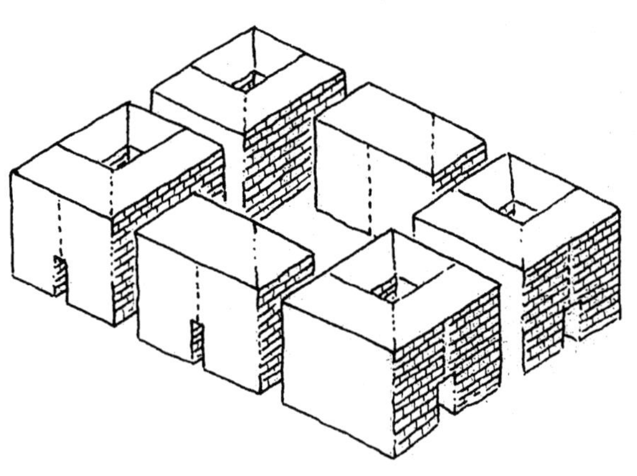

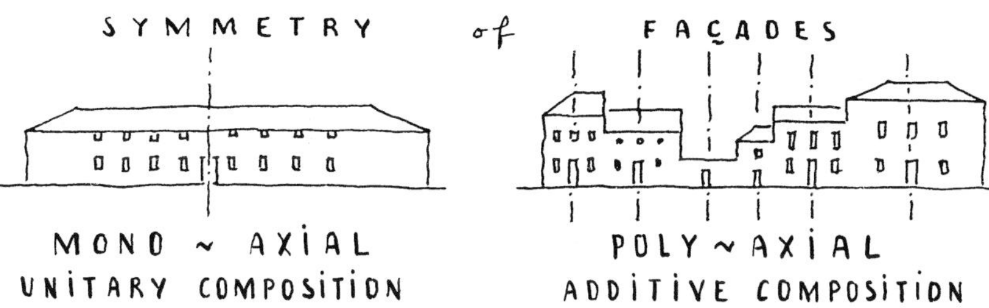
SYMMETRY of FAÇADES
MONO ~ AXIAL
UNITARY COMPOSITION
POLY ~ AXIAL
ADDITIVE COMPOSITION

ANIMATED FACADES
POOR PAVING
L.K. 87

POOR FACADES
AGITATED PAVING

NECESSITY of PROXIMITY

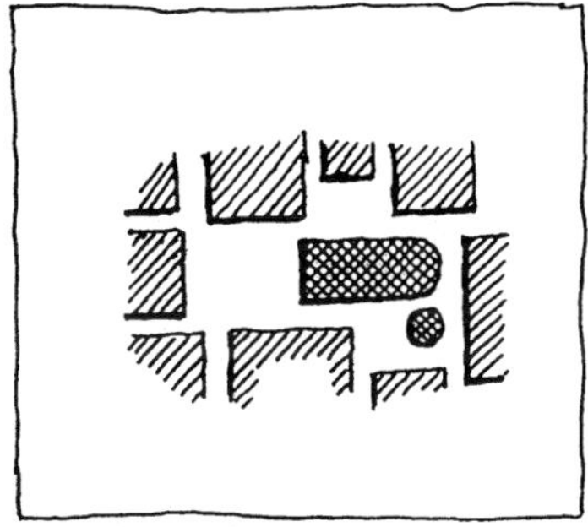

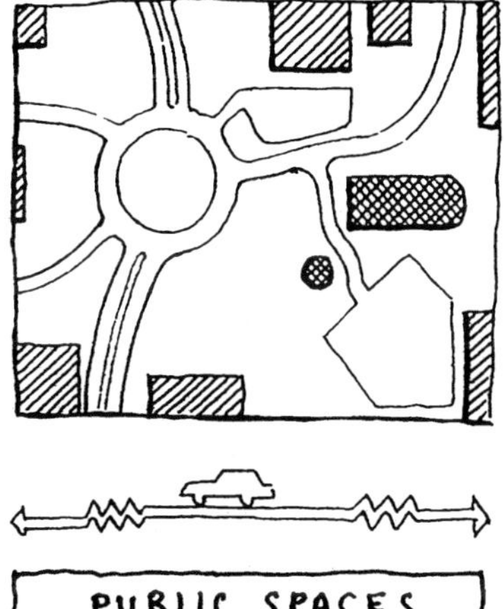

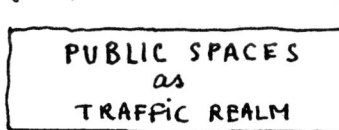

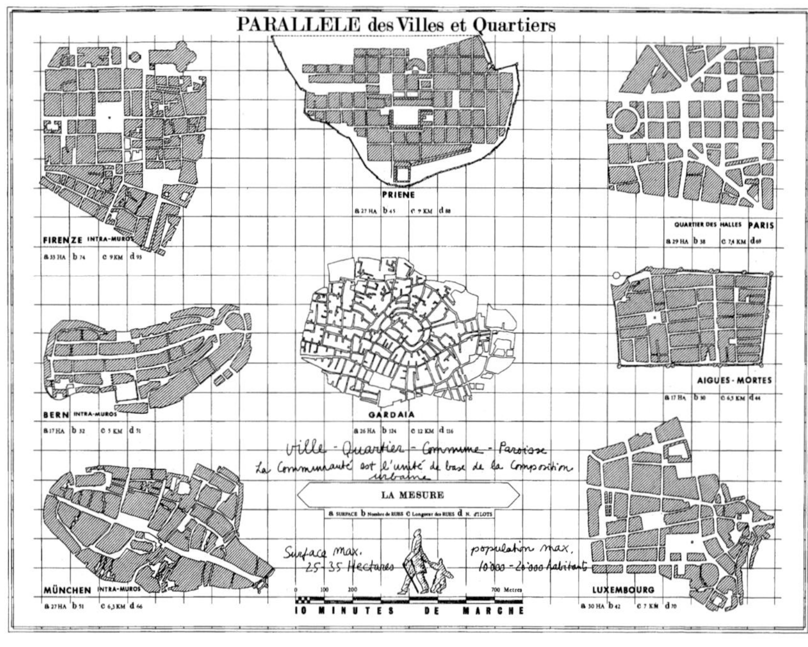
PARALLELE des Villes et Quartiers
PRIENE
a 27 HA b 45 c 9 KM d 88
FIRENZE INTRA-MUROS
a 33 HA b 74 c 9 KM d 93
QUARTIER DES HALLES PARIS
a 29 HA b 38 c 7,4 KM d 69
BERN INTRA-MUROS
a 17 HA b 32 c 5 KM d 51
GARDAIA
a 26 HA b 124 c 12 KM d 116
AIGUES - MORTES
a 17 HA b 30 c 6,5 KM d 44
Ville - Quartier - Commune - Paroisse
La Communauté est l'unité de base de la Composition urbaine
LA MESURE
a SURFACE b Nombre de RUES c Longueur des RUES d N. d'ILOTS
Surface max. 25-35 Hectares
population max. 10'000 - 20'000 habitants
0 100 200 700 Metres
10 MINUTES DE MARCHE
MÜNCHEN INTRA-MUROS
a 27 HA b 51 c 6,3 KM d 66
LUXEMBOURG
a 30 HA b 42 c 7 KM d 70

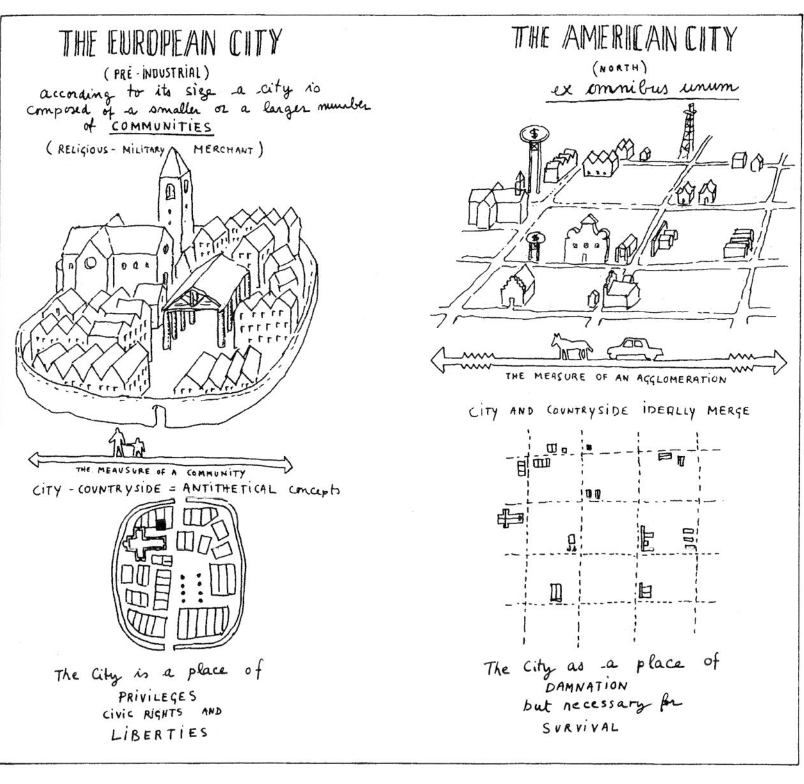
THE EUROPEAN CITY
(PRÉ-INDUSTRIAL)
according to its sige a city is composed of a smaller or a larger number of COMMUNITIES
(RELIGIOUS - MILITARY - MERCHANT)
THE MEAUSURE OF A COMMUNITY
CITY - COUNTRYSIDE = ANTITHETICAL concepts
The City is a place of
PRIVILEGES
CIVIC RIGHTS AND
LIBERTIES
THE AMERICAN CITY
(NORTH)
ex omnibus unum
THE MEASURE OF AN AGGLOMERATION
CITY AND COUNTRYSIDE IDEALLY MERGE
The City as a place of
DAMNATION
but necessary for
SURVIVAL

THE CITY OF LONDON
LK 86
A alternative futures

THE CITY OF LONDON
LK 86
B

SUSTAINABLE AND UNSUSTAINABLE BUILDING HEIGHTS

Low buildings & High Ceilings

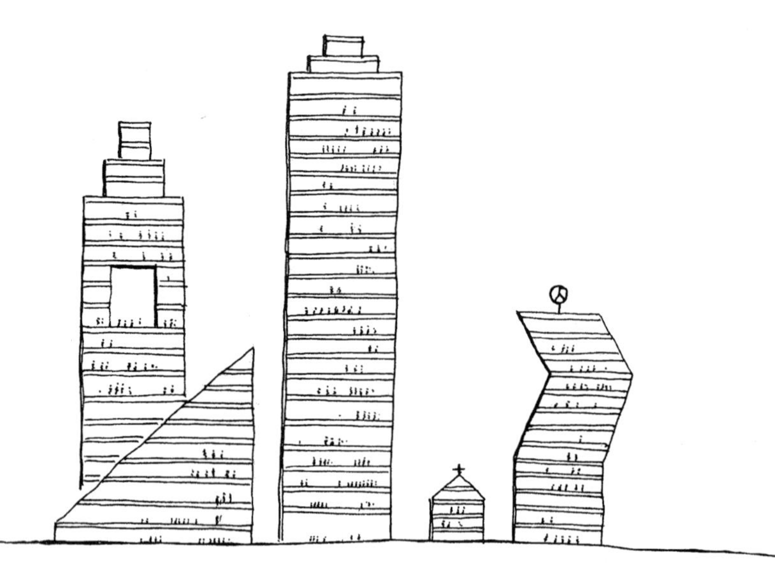

High buildings & Low ceilings

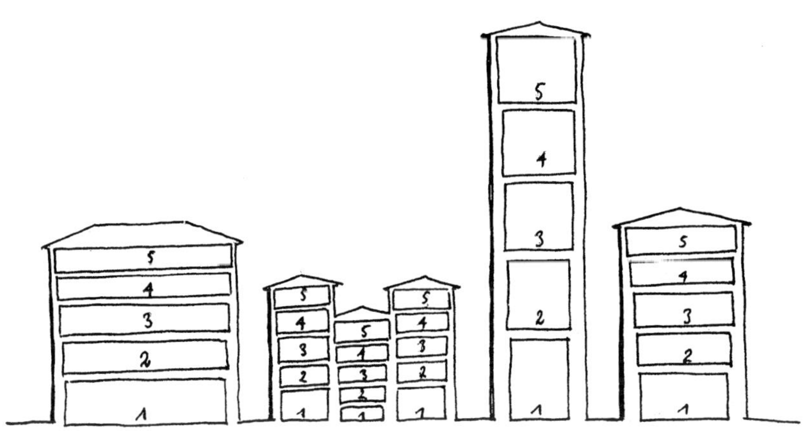

Limited Number of Floors

No height limit ~ Maximum Variation of Building's Ceiling height

VARIED SKYLINE

Limited Building Height

Maximum realisation of rentable floors ~ Minimum Ceiling height

UNIFORM SKYLINE

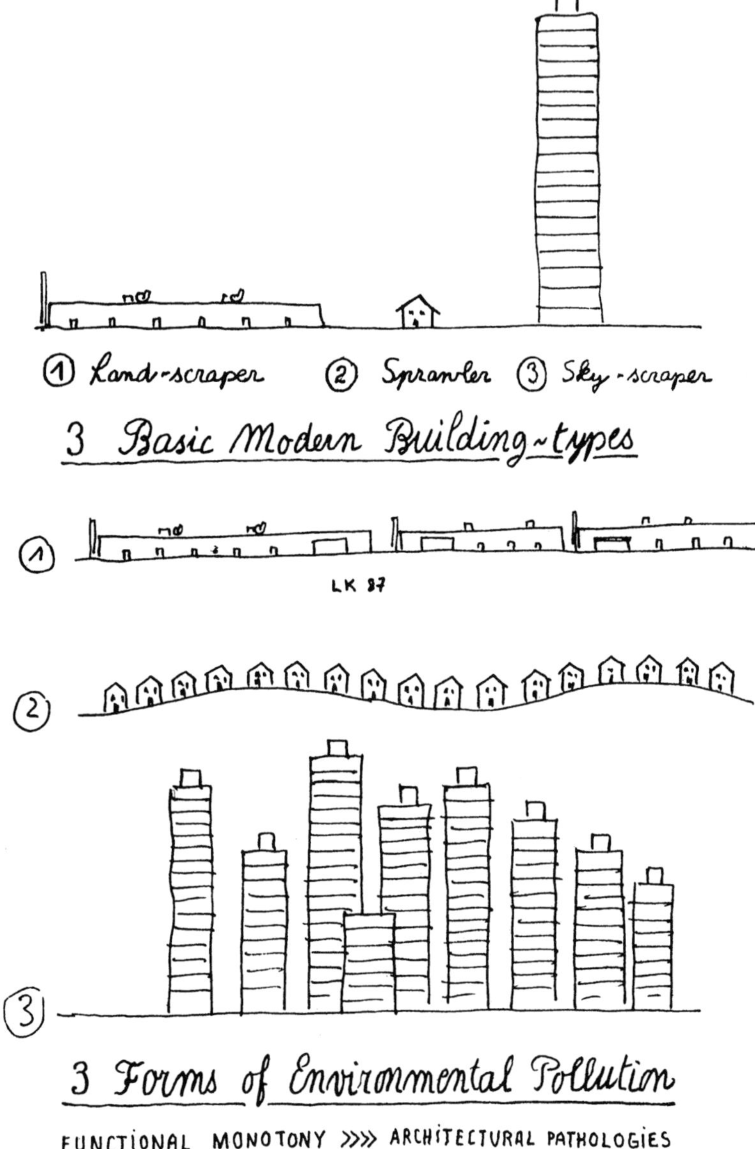

① Land-scraper
② Sprawler
③ Sky-scraper
3 Basic Modern Building-types
①
LK 87
②
③
3 Forms of Environmental Pollution
FUNCTIONAL MONOTONY >>>> ARCHITECTURAL PATHOLOGIES

MONOFUNCTIONAL ZONING ⟹ MEGASTRUCTURES

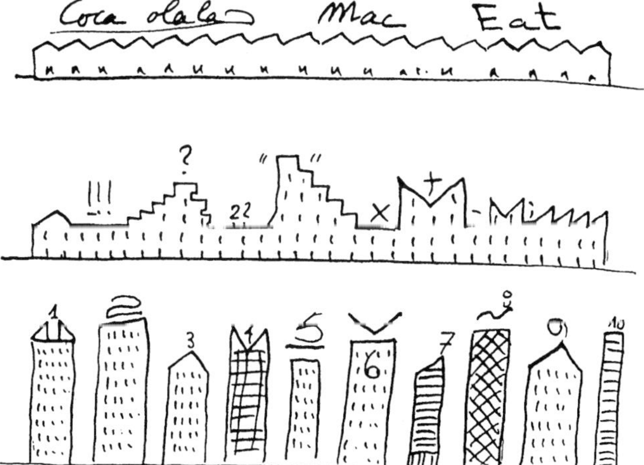

PETER PAN SCENARIO

till when?

? BUILT OUT PEAK ?

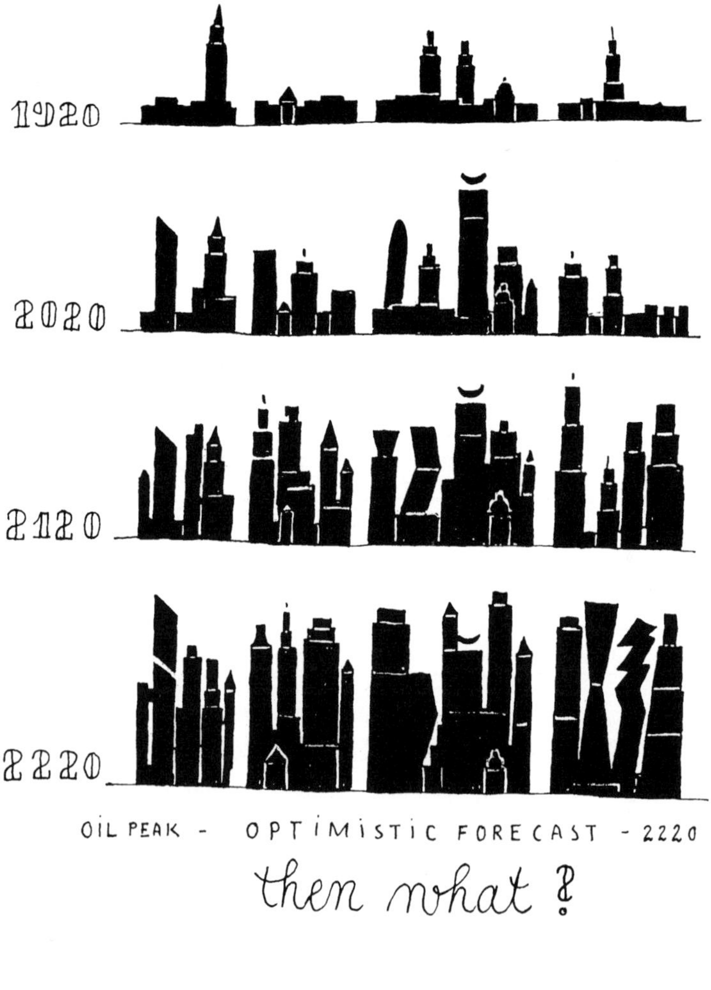

1920

2020

2120

2220

OIL PEAK - OPTIMISTIC FORECAST - 2220

then what?

Long Term effects of excessive Plot-Ratio ordinances

Manhattan Logic

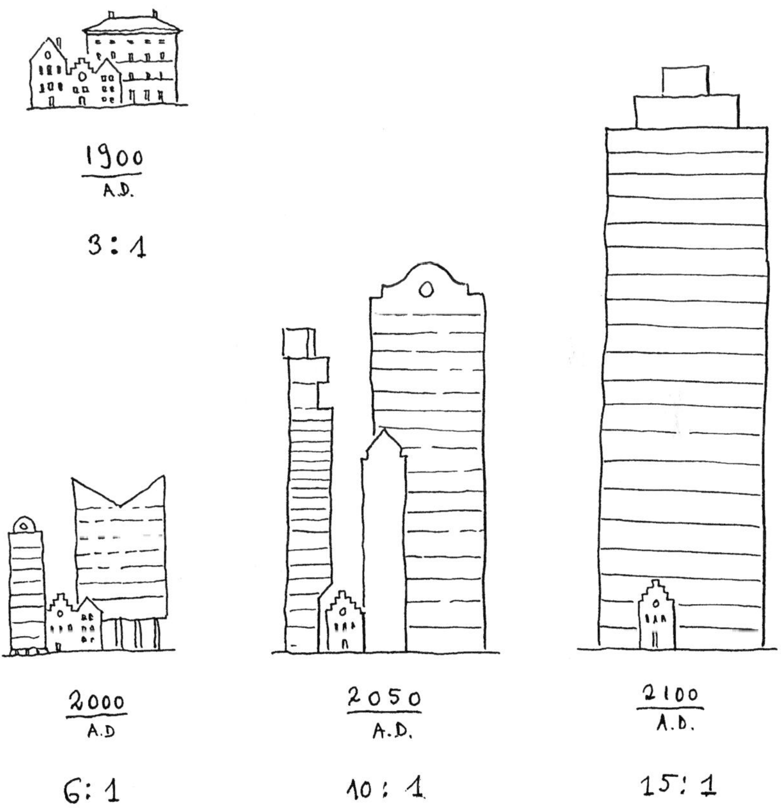

THE FATAL LOVE ~ STORY

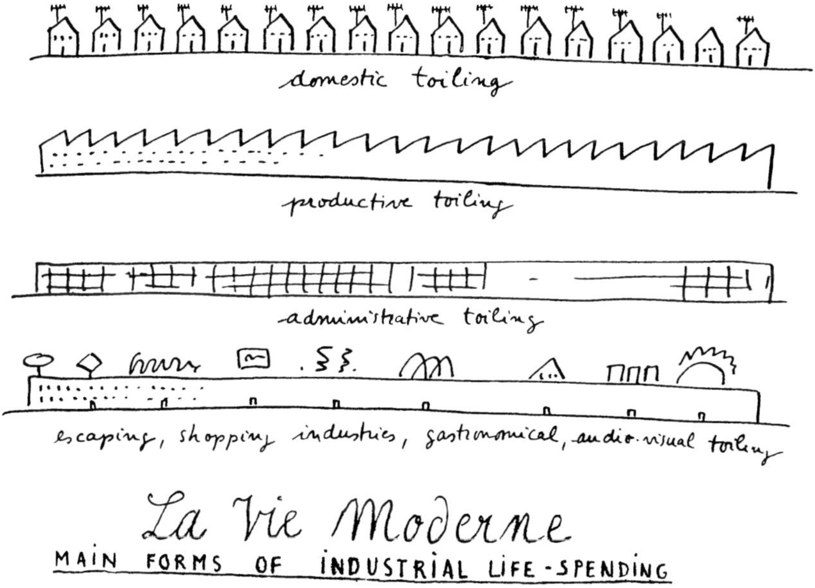

domestic toiling

productive toiling

administrative toiling

escaping, shopping industries, gastronomical, audio-visual toiling

La Vie Moderne

MAIN FORMS OF INDUSTRIAL LIFE-SPENDING

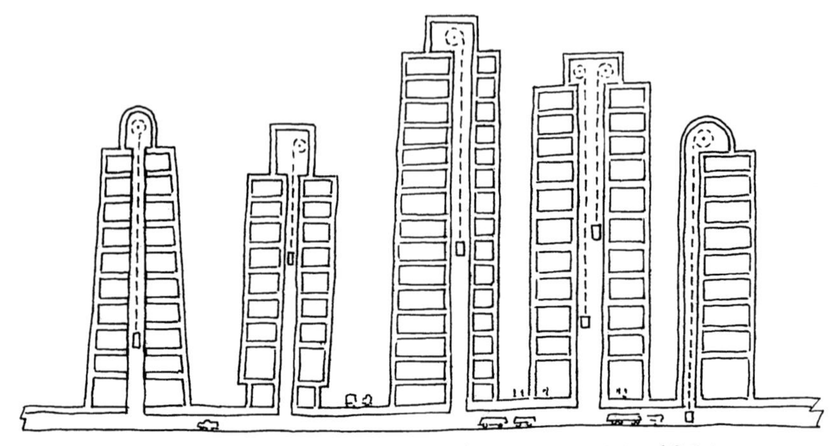

SKYSCRAPERS as VERTICAL CUL-DE-SACS or NETWORK CONGESTORS

2 MAIN NETWORK 'CONGESTORS'

(Network killers and parasites)

L.K. 04

VERTICAL HORIZONTAL

CUL-DE-SACS

architectural
PRIAPISM
(no cure known)

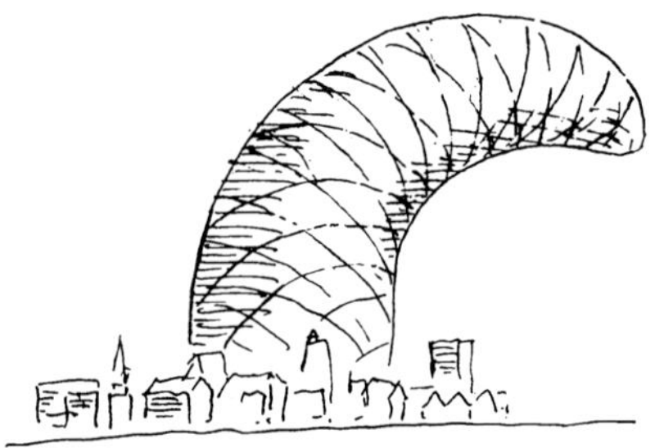

THE TOWER ~ DRIVE

controled ~ uncontroled

TOWER-LESS SPRAWL "towerless"

FUTURELESS HORIZONTALITY

TRUE SKYSCRAPER CITY "tower-ful"

HORIZONTAL CITY WITH VERTICAL ACCENTS

LK 06

SPRAWLING TOWERS "tower-sick"

FUTURELESS VERTICALITY

TUNING BUILDINGS AND URBAN FABRIC

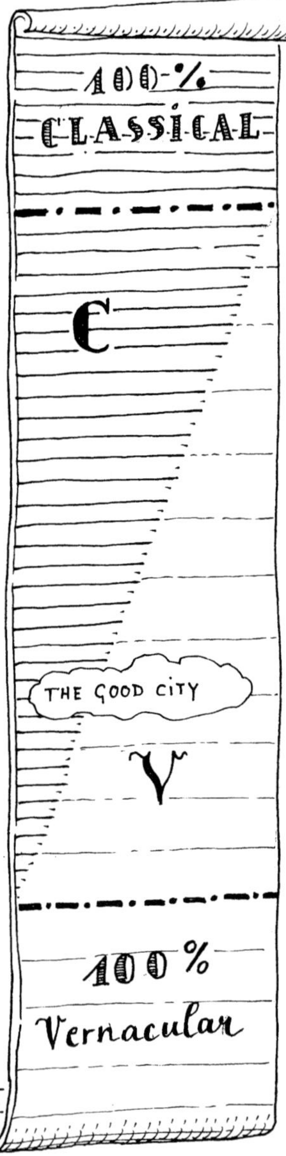
HOW MUCH CLASSICAL & Vernacular IS NEEDED TO MAKE THE GOOD CITY?
100%
CLASSICAL
C
THE GOOD CITY
V
100%
Vernacular
BEAUX-ARTS UTOPIA
CHICAGO WHITE CITY 1893
VERSAILLES CASTLE + PARK
NAPOLEON III - VICTORIANA
IMPERIALISME
ROME CAMPO MARTIO
FORBIDDEN CITY BEJING
ACROPOLIS
RENAISSANCE IDEAL CITIES
VENICE
ROTHENBURG O.T.
CESKY-KRUMLOV
ATHENS CLASSICAL AGE
WILLIAMSBURG
TRADITIONAL VILLAGES
PRIMORDIAL HAMLETS
LASCAUX
ANIMAL ARCHITECTURE

TUNING OF URBAN NETWORK & ARCHITECTURE

©LK 03

URBAN. [U] URBANISM • NETWORK OF PUPLIC ROUTES & SPACES

ARCH. [A] ARCHITECTURE • PUBLIC/CIVIC — PRIVATE DOMESTIC

VERN. [V] VERNACULAR • INFORMAL - ORGANIC GEOMETRY - PROSE

CLASS. [C] CLASSICAL • FORMAL - EUCLIDEAN GEOMETRY - POETRY

I	URB. VERN. ARCH. VERN.	UV AV	• VILLAGES • HAMLETS • PUEBLOS • • FARMS • "ENSEMBLES SPONTANÉS" • PORT-GRIMAUD •
II	URB. VERN. ARCH. CLASS	UV AC	• ATHENS ACROPOLIS • AGORA • REPUBLICAN FORUM ROME • OLYMPIA • NARA TEMPLES • MONTI SACRI
III	URB. VERN. ARCH. VERN. + CLASS.	UV AV+C	• VENEZIA • LUCCA • UZES • • SAN GIMIGNANO • ÎLE DE LA CITÉ • • ROTHENBURG • DINKELSBÜHL • SIENA • ASSOS • BELLAGGIO • SEVILLE
IV	URB. CLASS. ARCH. VERN.	UC AV	• BARRACKS • CONCENTRATION CAMPS • • PRISONS • "VILLE RADIEUSE" • • HILBERSEIMER BERLIN • INDUSTRIAL UTOPIAS • • SPANISH ENSANCHES • NEW DEAL HOUSING •
V	URB. CLASS. ARCH. CLASS.	UC AC	• IMPERIAL CAPITALS • BATH • VERSAILLES • • BABYLON • KARNAK • FORBIDDEN CITY • RENAISSANCE UTOPIAS • BEAUX-ARTS • TURIN • • HAUSSMAN-PARIS • SPEER-GERMANIA •
VI	URB. CLASS. ARCH. VERN + CLASS.	UC AV+C	• PRIENE • TIMGAD • KYOTO • WINDSOR FL. • • CHARLOTTESVILLE • WILLIAMSBURG • • YALE CAMPUS • JEFFERSON GRID • • SALINES DE CHAUX • LAW OF INDIES • BASTIDES TOWNS • FIRENZVOLA
VII	URB. VERN. + CLASS. ARCH. VERN.	UV+C AV	• HAMPSTEAD GARDEN SUBURB • • SUBURBIA • • MODERNIST NEW TOWNS • UK • FRANCE • • USSR • CHINA • BRASILIA •
VIII	URB. VERN. + CLASS ARCH. CLASS.	UV+C AC	• PALMYRA • LEPTIS • CHANTILLY CASTLE • RESIDENZ STÄDTE SCHWETZINGEN • POTSDAM • • VATICAN-CITY • CESKY-KRUMLOV • • BORDEAUX • KREMLIN •
IX	URB. VERN. + CLASS. ARCH. VERN. + CLASS.	UV+C AV+C	• PIENZA • NOLLI-ROME • PRAGUE • ISE • ISTANBUL • CAIRO • DRESDEN • CUSCO • SAMARKAND • KATMANDU • LHASSA • NEW URBANISM • POUNDBURY

TUNING OF URBAN ARCHITECTURE
«TUA»

URBANISM

VERNACULAR | CLASSICAL | VERNACULAR+CLASSICAL

ARCHITECTURE

VERNACULAR

CLASSICAL

VERNACULAR & CLASSICAL

LK © 03

TUNING OF URBAN ARCHITECTURE
«TUA»

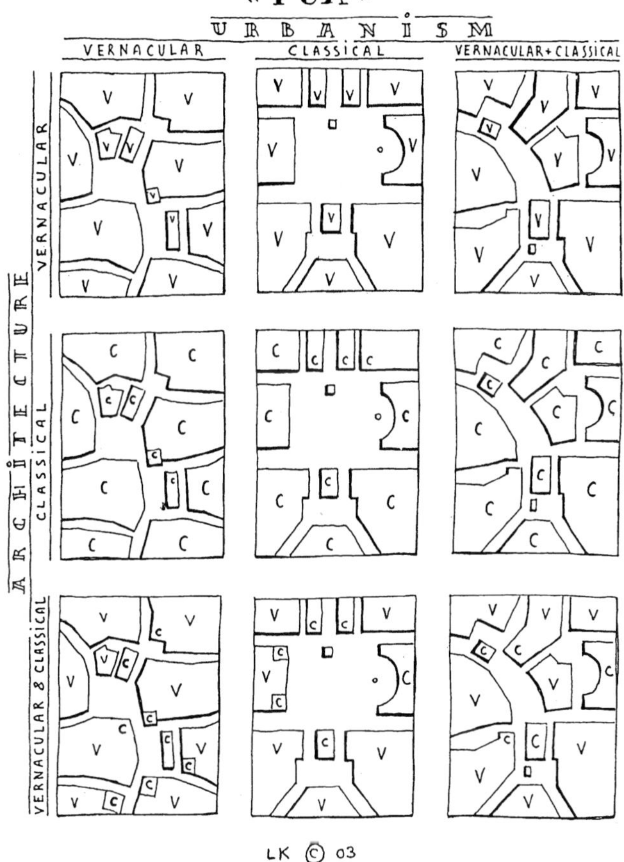

CHART OF PERMUTATIONS

CHARTS OF PERMUTATIONS

I	IV	VII
II	V	VIII
III	VI	IX

	UV	UC	UC+V
AV	UV AV	UC AV	UVC AV
AC	UV AC	UC AC	UVC AC
AV+C	UV AVC	UC AVC	UVC AVC

QUALITY OF ARCH. DOSAGE

PP MISMATCH
P POOR
S SATISFACTORY
I IDEAL
G GOOD
GG NECESSARY

S	PP	P
G	GG	S
G	S	I

TO MAKE a CITY

MIXED USE

IS NECESSARY BUT NOT SUFFICIENT

a condition

I

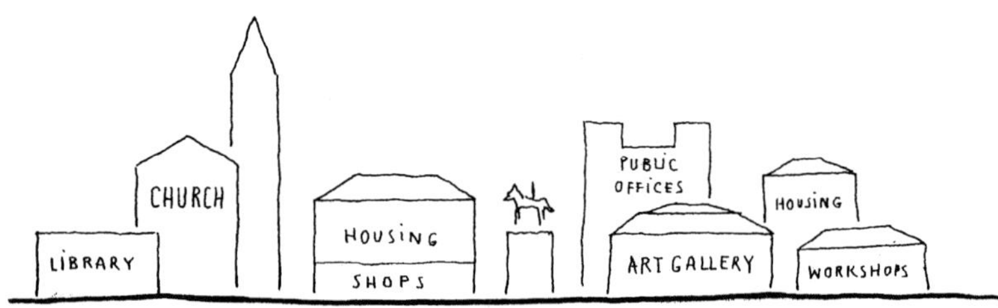

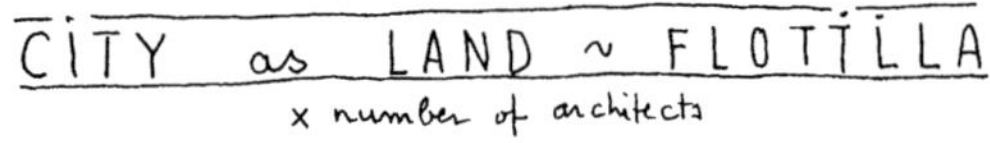

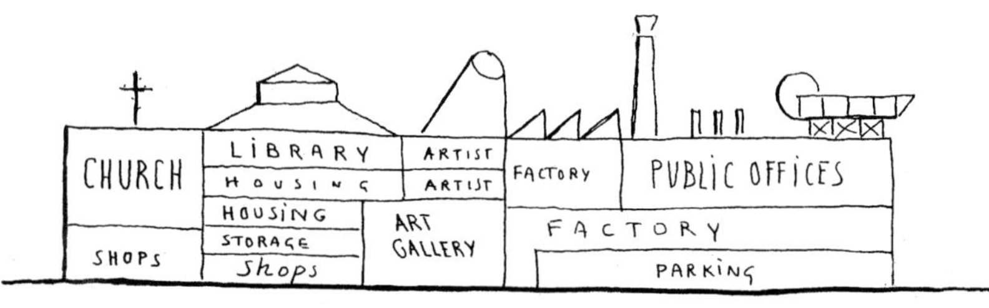

TO MAKE a CITY

MIXED USE

IS a NECESSARY BUT NOT A SUFFICIENT condition

II

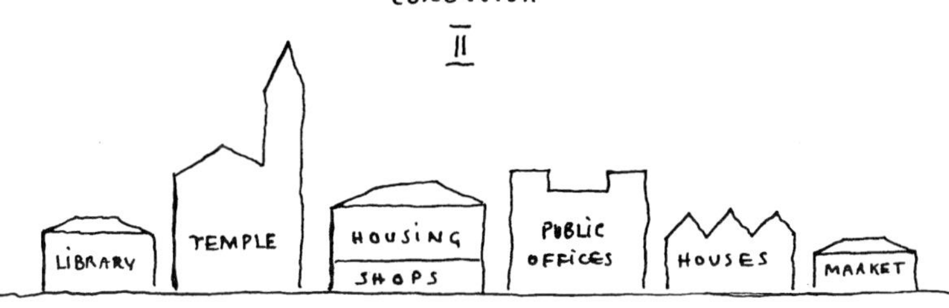

TYPOLOGICAL ORDER
FUNCTIONAL = ARCHITECTURAL VARIETY

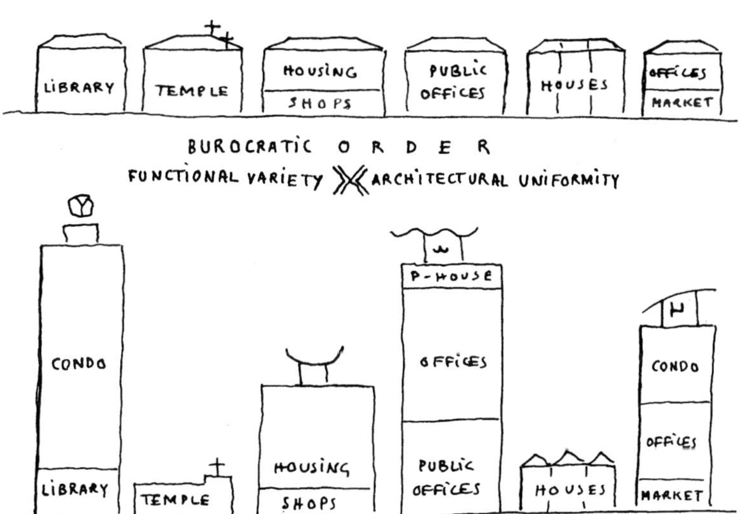

OVERDEVELOPMENT - MANHATTANISM
FUNCTIONAL VARIETY X ARCHITECTURAL VARIETY

ARCHITECTURAL TUNING OF URBAN COMPOSITION

<vernacular & CLASSICAL>

vernacularissimus

AUSTERITY VERNACULAR

vernacular & CLASSICAL

CULTURAL APOGEE

CLASSICÍSSIMUS

IMPERIAL CARNIVAL CLASSICISM

L.K. 06

APPLYING & SIZING OF CLASSICAL and vernacular MODES

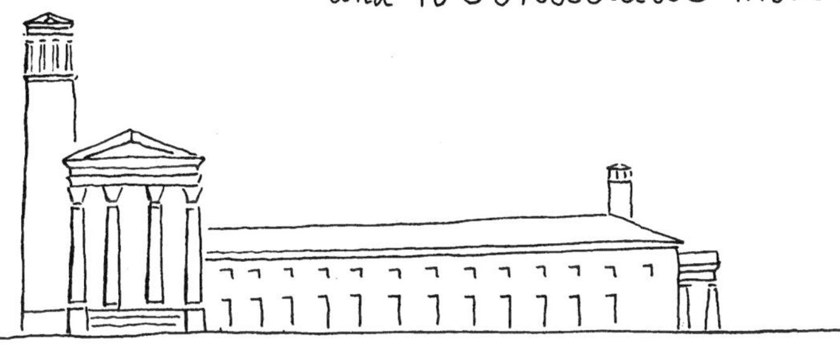

well-applied & well-sized

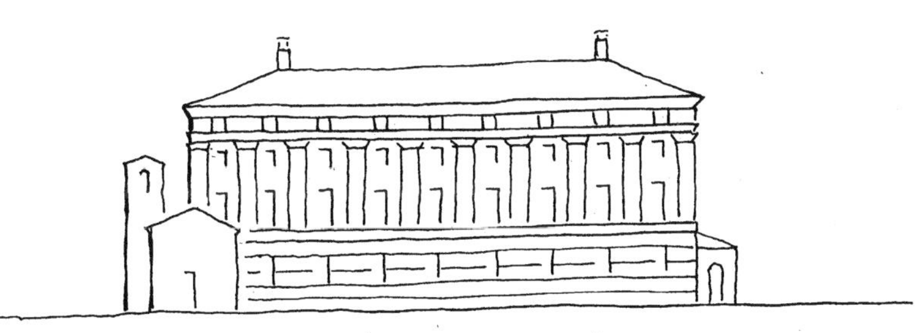

mis-applied & mis-sized

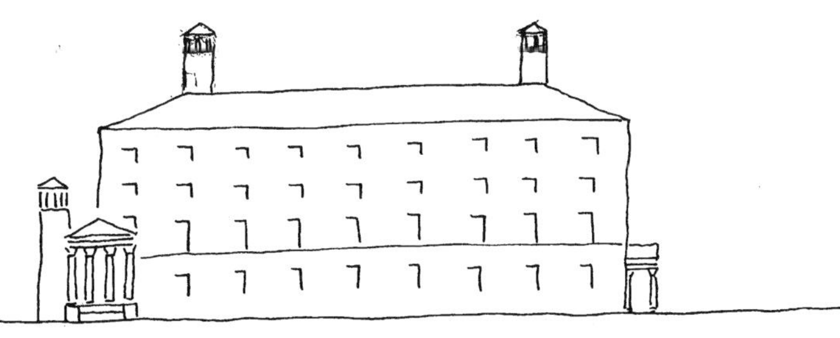

well-applied & mis-sized

LK 05

PRIVATE IMPERIALISM
GOOD PRIVATE / PUBLIC AFFAIRS
PUBLIC IMPERIALISM
LK 03

architectural SPEECH

architectural STUTTER

LK 99

FORMS AND UNIFORMS

TYPE & MODEL (A) INDUSTRIAL (B) FINE ARTS – CRAFTS / NATURE

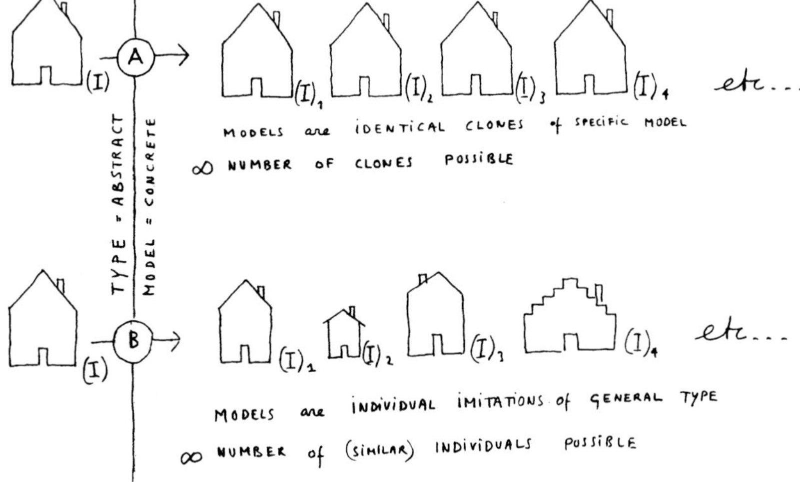

GEOLOGIC FORM ~ CHANGE THROUGH EROSION

"nature"

TECTONIC FORM ~ PERMANENCE THROUGH ARCHITECTURE

EROSION MASTERED BY TECHNICAL ARTIFICE

ANALOGICAL IMITATION of nature

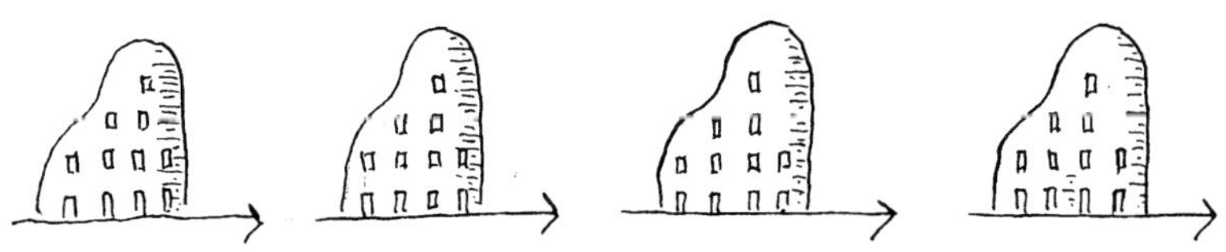

GEOLOGIC FORM SIMULACRUM ~ FROZEN EROSION

EROSION CHECKED IN ERODED FORM

MECHANICAL IMITATION of nature

TYPOLOGIES of ROOMS or CORRIDORS

of cellular or arterial structures

not to be confused EVER AGAIN!!!!! please

DOMINANT VOLUME & ROOM CORRESPOND
perceivable at one glance

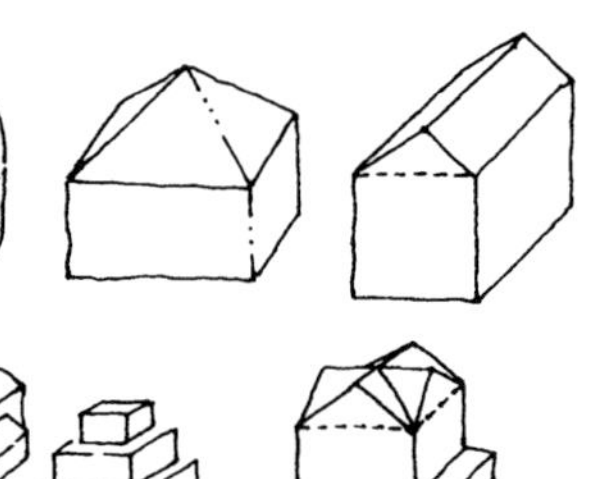

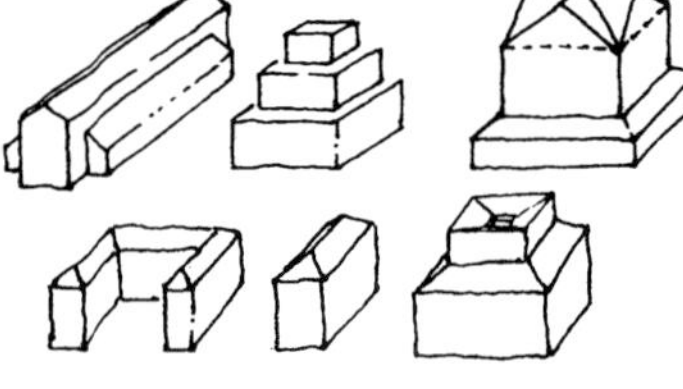

BUILDINGS AS LABYRINTHINE
circulation structures

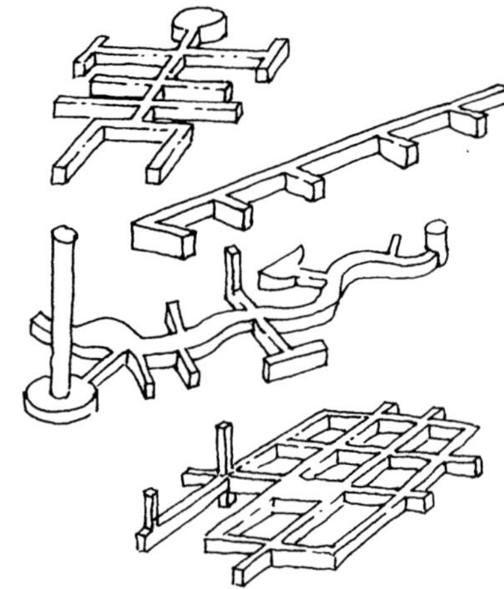

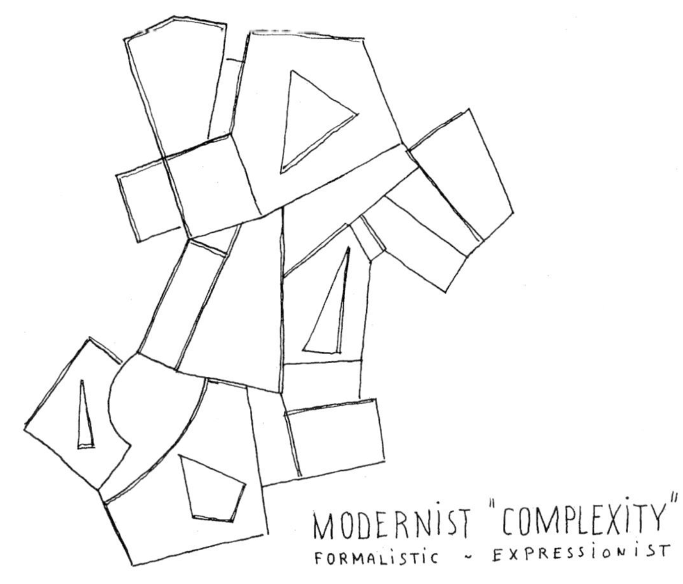
MODERNIST "COMPLEXITY"
FORMALISTIC ~ EXPRESSIONIST

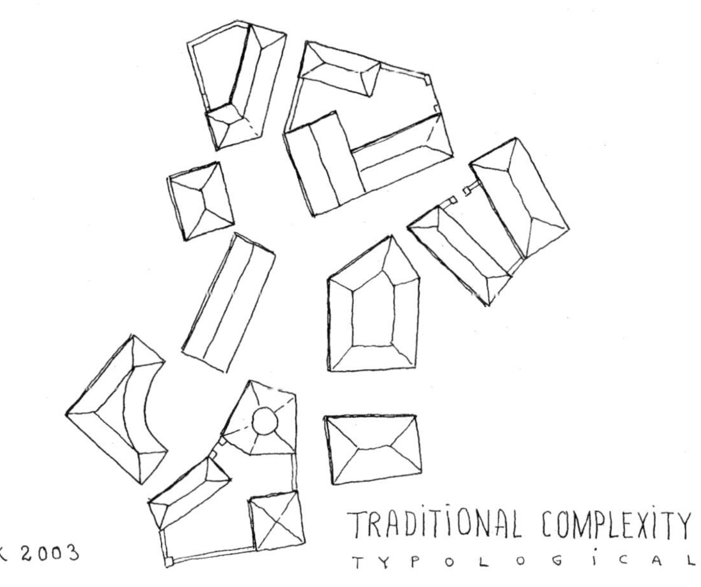
TRADITIONAL COMPLEXITY
TYPOLOGICAL
LK 2003

UNIFORM

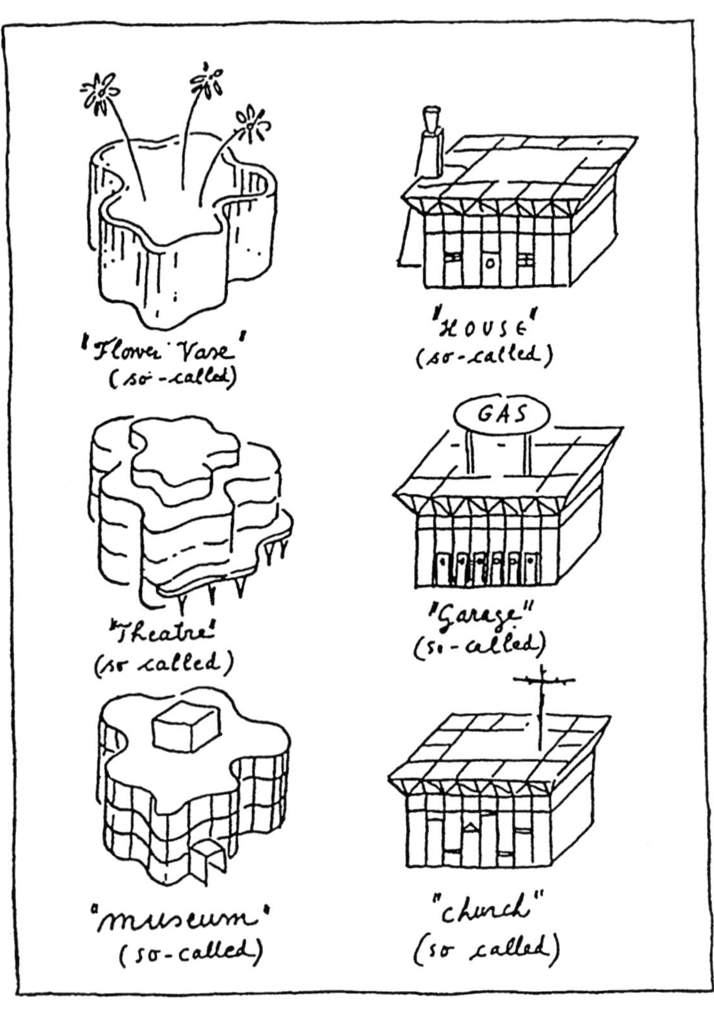

SO~CALLED "OBJECTS"

versus FORM

NAMEABLE OBJECTS

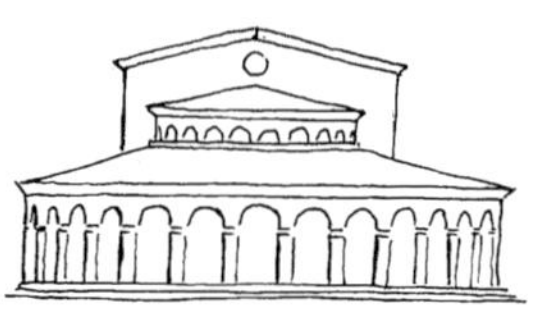

DOMESTIC & CIVIC × SCALE × QUALITATIVE OR QUANTITATIVE   LK 03

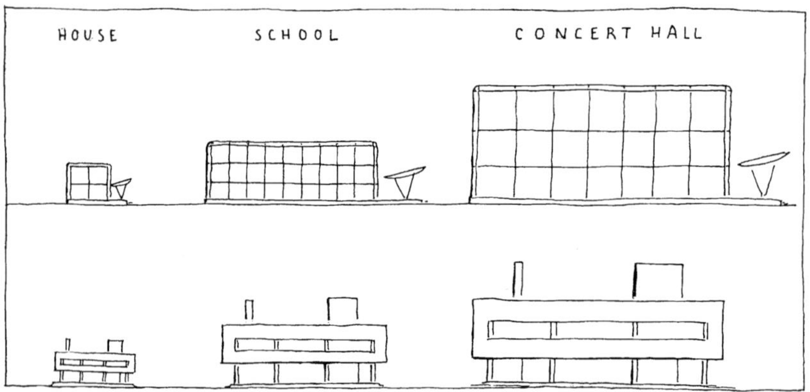

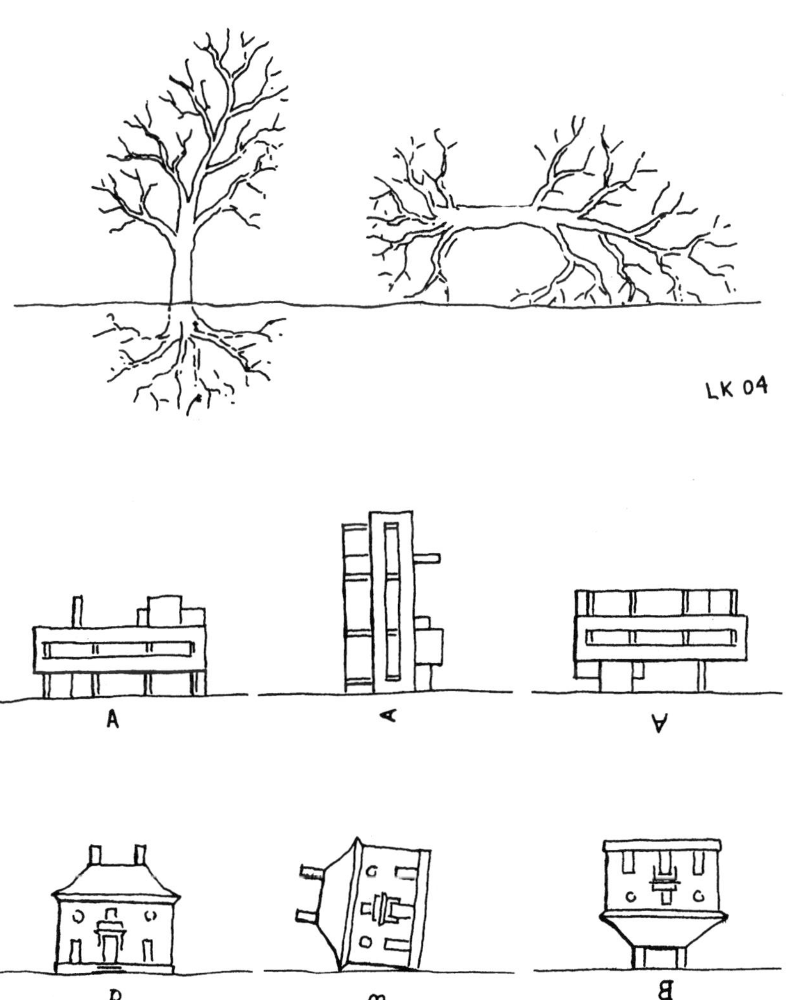
DON'T FORGET YOUR GRAVITY CHECK
LK 04
A
A
A
B
B
B

OBJETS
TYPES
· U S E ·
PASTICHES
· CONSUMPTION ·
CHURCH
COUNTRY HOUSE
MOSQUE
PUMPING - STATION
POWER STATION
PALACE of CULTURE
SHIP
CLUB
WARE - HOUSE
CHAPELLE
USINE
PARLIAMENT
TRADITION
FORM = CONTENT
HISTORICISMODERNISM
CONTENT X FORM

RANDOM UNIFORMITY

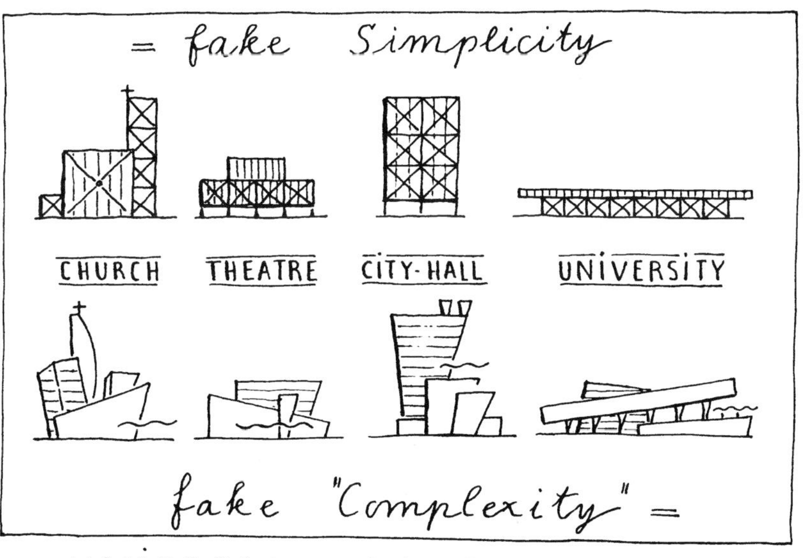

UNIFORM RANDOMNESS

This school must not be composed like a single building with one entrance

TWO KINDS OF MONSTERS

AUTHORITARIAN LOOK

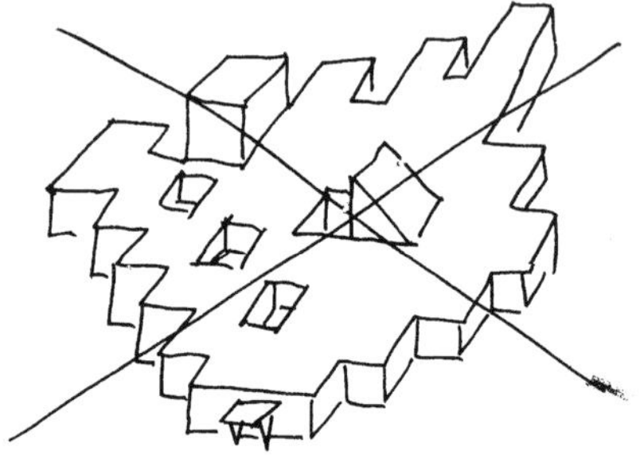

DEMOCRATIC LOOK

This school will be composed like a city with small and big buildings according to their importance

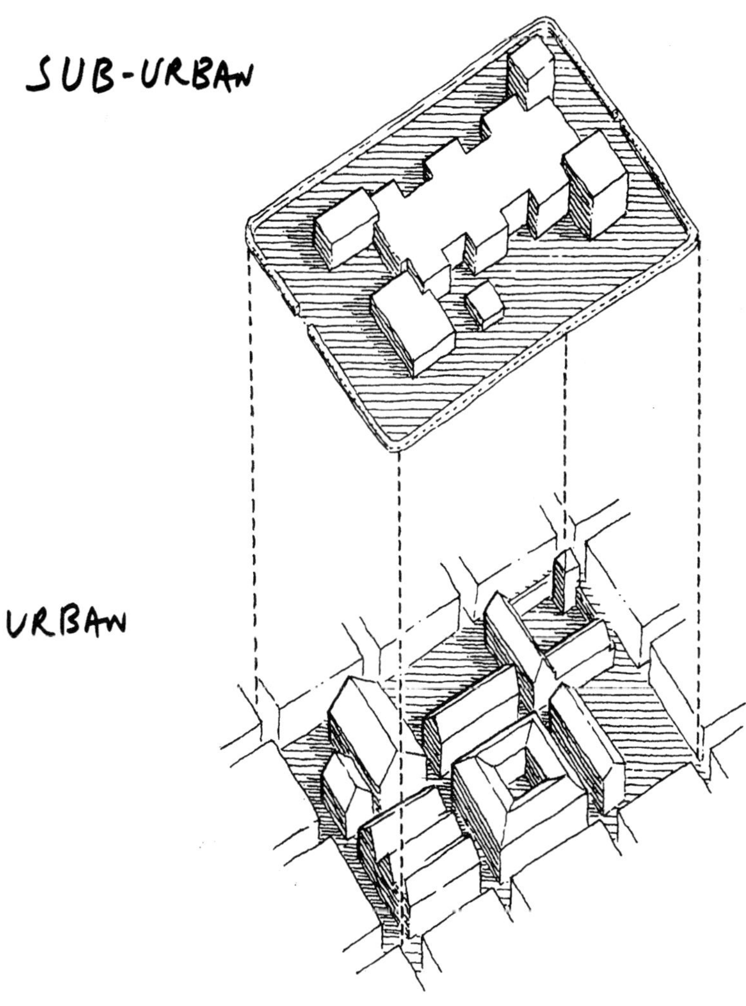

SCHOOL + civic center buildings

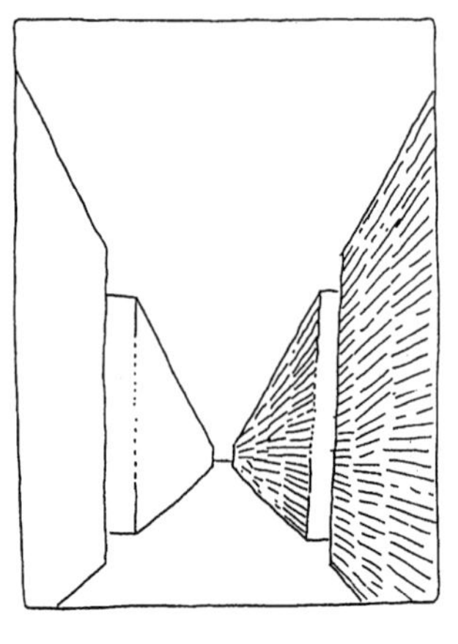

UN-FOCUSED

FOCUSED

STREET

As CORRIDOR

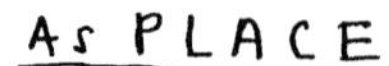

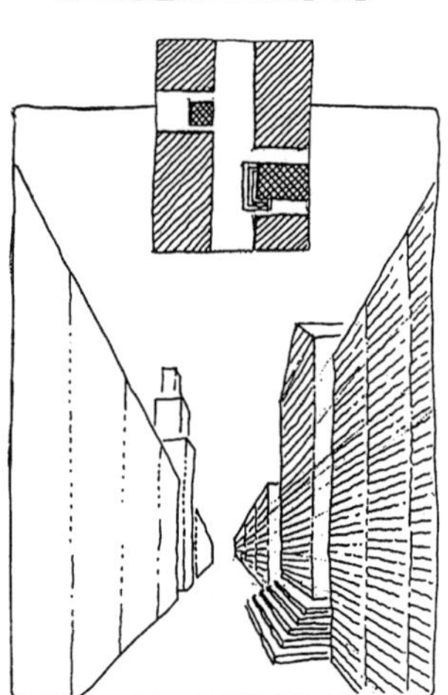

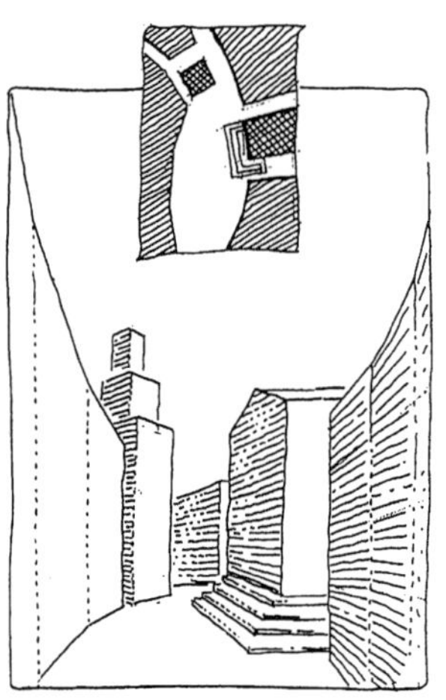

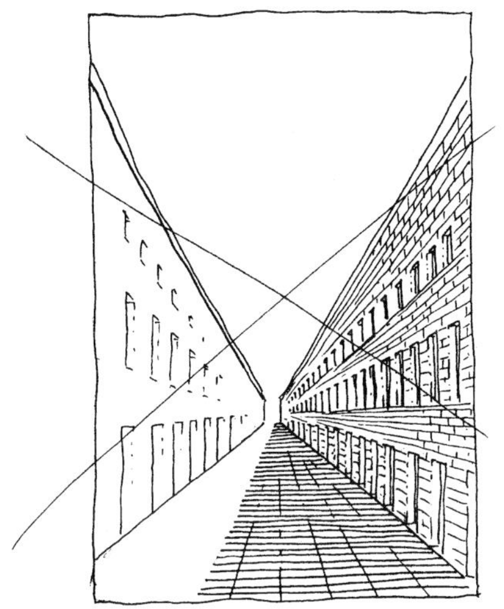

The Prison

Two Streets

The city

CONSERVATION AND MAINTENANCE

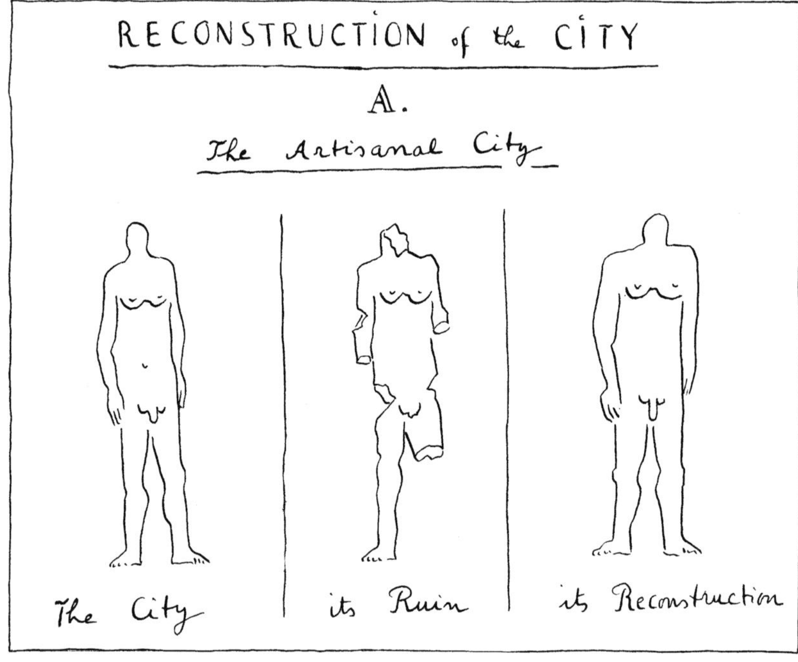
RECONSTRUCTION of the CITY
A.
The Artisanal City
The City
its Ruin
its Reconstruction

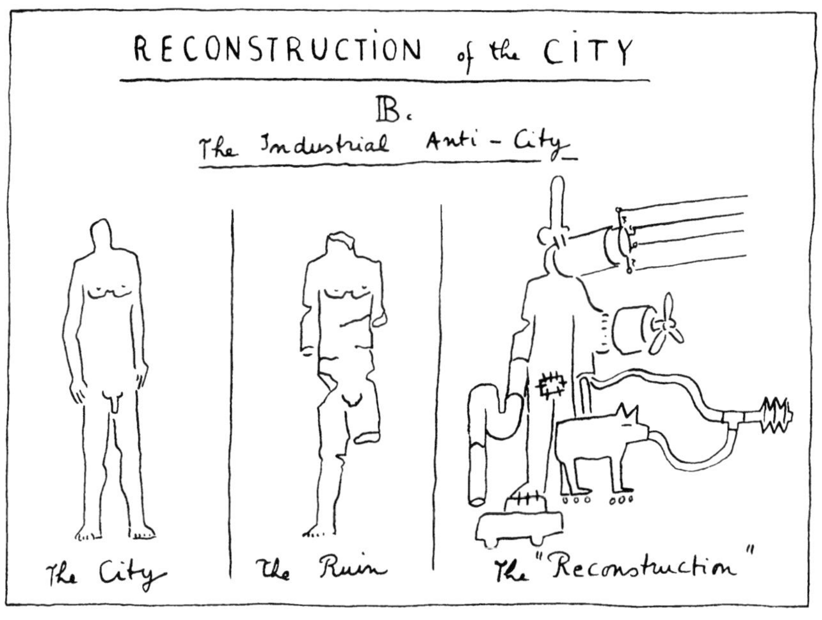
RECONSTRUCTION of the CITY
B.
The Industrial Anti-City
The City
The Ruin
The "Reconstruction"

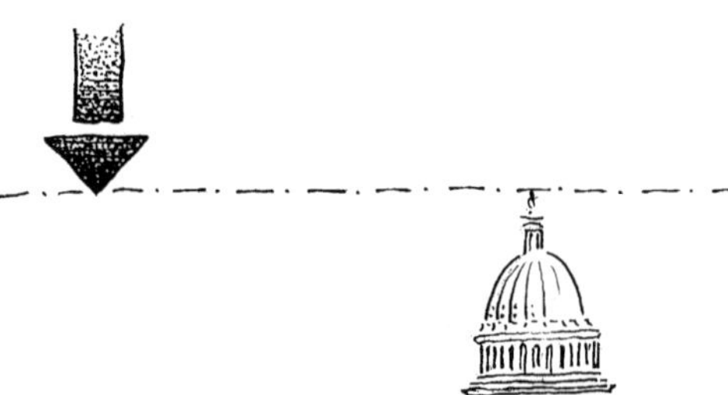

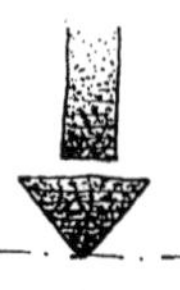

UNACCEPTABLE LIMITATIONS

ON

THE CAPITALS SKYLINE

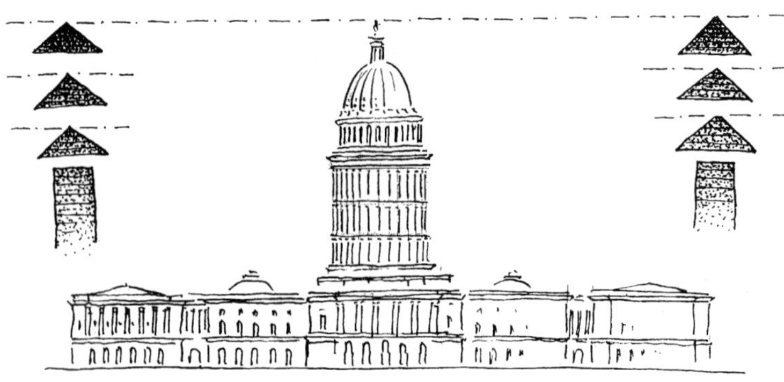

THE "UPWARD SOLUTION"

NEGOTIABLE

LK 04

1990
RUIN
HISTORIC 100 M
NO PHOTO OPPORTUNITY

400 B.C.
LK 05
PHOTO OPPORTUNITY

LK 85
Ex ~ tensions

Conservative versus Creative Restauration

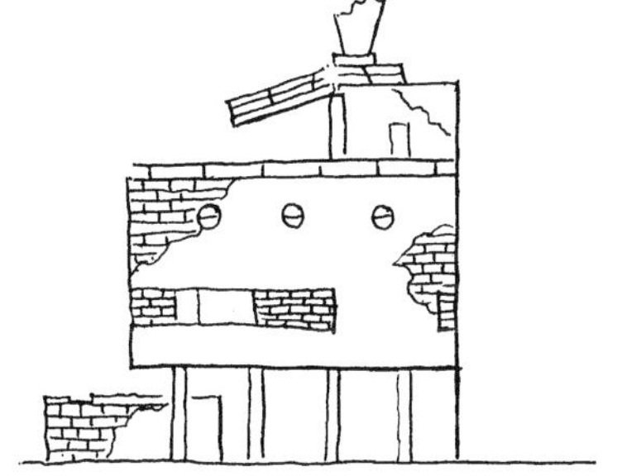

Derelict Modernist Masterpiece

Conservative Restauration (Nostalgic)

Creative (forward looking) Restauration

Respect through Contrast

Reichstag

Villa Savoye

"Charter of Venice" and "Conservation has gone too far" principles ecumenically applied.

LK 99

Charter of Venice applied to the restoration of Gozzoli-fresco
LK 1986

Though an Act of Parliament can abolish the GLC, it can't abolish the wishes of Londoners to have their own elected authority.*

Not now, not ever.

And because there's no time like the present for thinking about the future, the GLC is undertaking a research project into the likely options a new government for London could take.

Typically, it's based on the views and opinions of Londoners – from professional organisations to voluntary bodies to individuals alike.

Which means we'd like to hear from you. We'd welcome any comments, be they criticisms or suggestions.

To help you, we've put together a special leaflet. It tells you how London has been run in the past, how it is run now and how it could be run in the future.

To obtain the leaflet, simply send off the coupon. But do give it some thought. After all, it is your future we're talking about.

FUTURE OF LONDON'S GOVERNMENT

Please send me a leaflet to

NAME

ADDRESS

Send to: London Research Project, DG/FLG, Room B9, FREEPOST, London SE1 7BP.
Or tel: 633 5427

GLC
Working for London

Due to demand, the deadline for submissions has been extended to 31.1.86.

G.L.C. PROPAGANDA UNIT 1985

GUESS WHO OFFERED YOU NO SAY IN THE PAST GOVERNMENT FOR LONDON.

This is what the GLC did to the Greater Part of London.

Londoners look at your city!!

L.K. OPINION 1985

Conservation versus Over-Development

PRESERVED HISTORIC CITY

HISTORIC PRESERVATION VIA LIFT-OFF

LK 2005

BEAUTIFUL PARTS

STABLE × ASSEMBLAGE × UNSTABLE

SUSTAINABLE UNSUSTAINABLE

MAINTENANCE & CULTURE

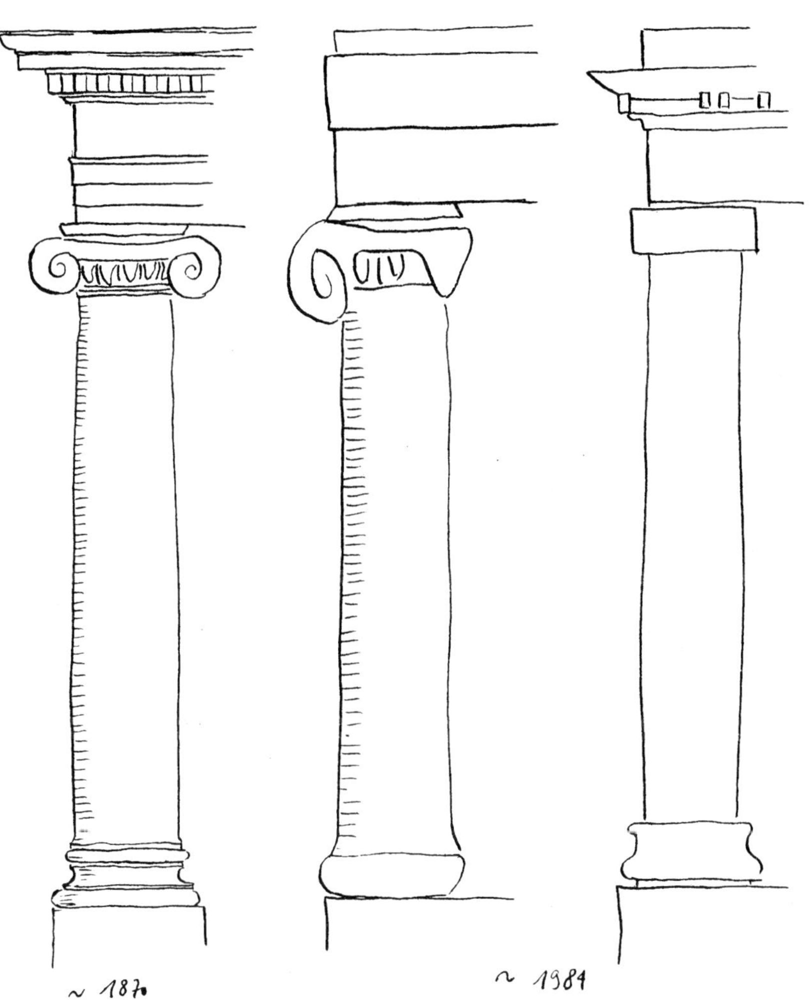

from CLASSICAL to vernacular
observed in Belsize Park - London

(YALE UNIVERSITY) BUILDINGS-AGE
AND FIRST MAJOR MAINTENANCE
CAMPAIGNS

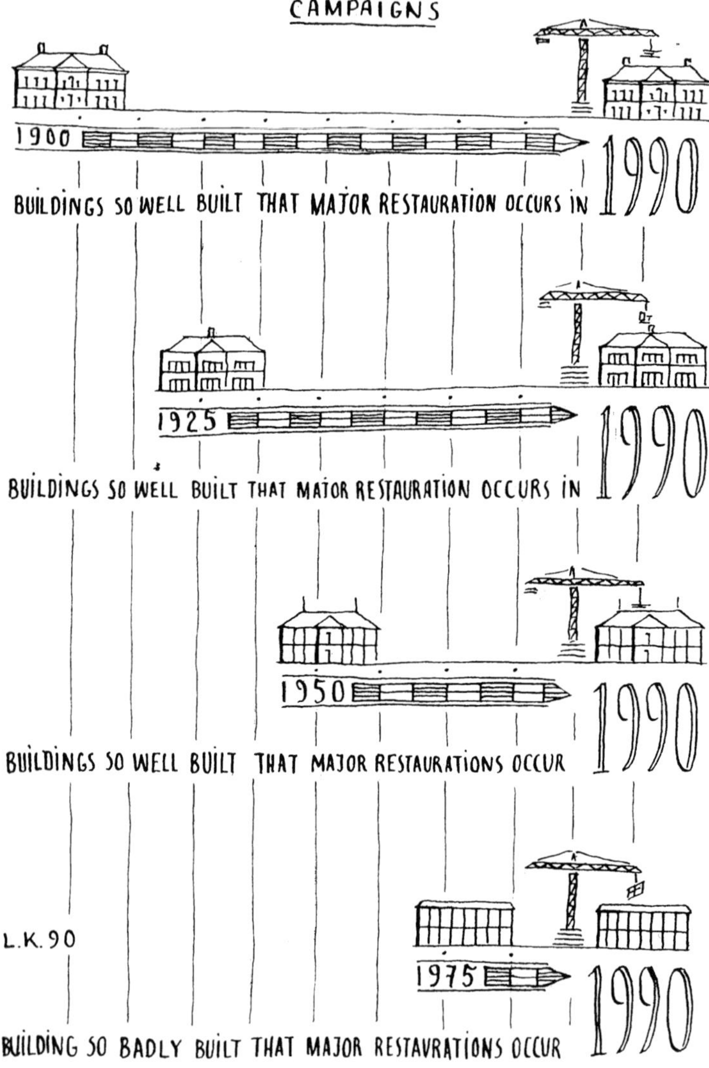

COTTAGE STUDIO
FOR AYN RAND
FRANK LEON ROARK
COTTAGE STUDIO
FOR AYN RAND
FRANK LLOYD WRIGHT

ARCHITECTURAL PATHOLOGIES

Genealogy of the House
30 A.D.
1030 A.D.
1830 A.D.
1930 A.D.
2030 A.D.
TEMPORARY REFUSAL of the ARCHETYPE
LK 88

HOUSE

HOUSES
LK 82

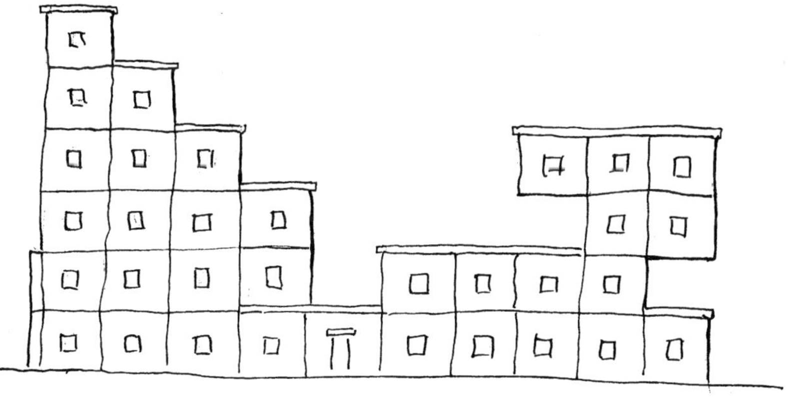
HOUSING

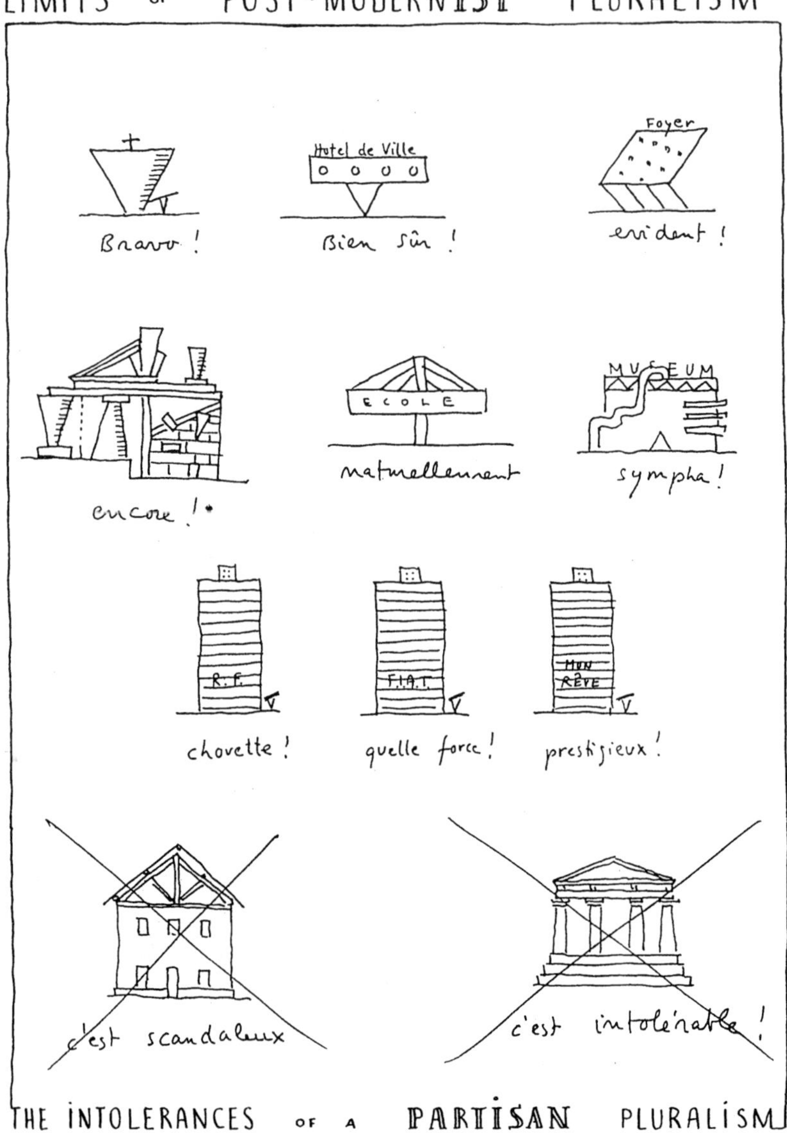
LIMITS OF POST-MODERNIST "PLURALISM"
Hotel de Ville
Foyer
Bravo!
Bien sûr!
évident!
ECOLE
MUSEUM
encore!*
naturellement
sympa!
R.F.
F.I.A.T.
MON RÊVE
chouette!
quelle force!
prestigieux!
c'est scandaleux
c'est intolérable!
THE INTOLERANCES OF A PARTISAN PLURALISM

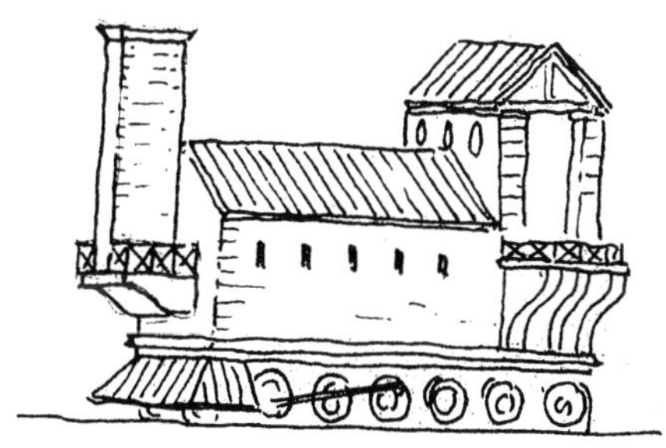

"INNOVATION = CONFUSION OF GENRE"

Let us suppose that one day an innovation fever was to befall engineers and would dictate them to abandon the means of their profession; would it then, I ask you, be less idiotic to ask the traveller to design his own aeroplane than it is to ask the inhabitant to invent the form of his house?

Award-winning Villa
before
Earthquake

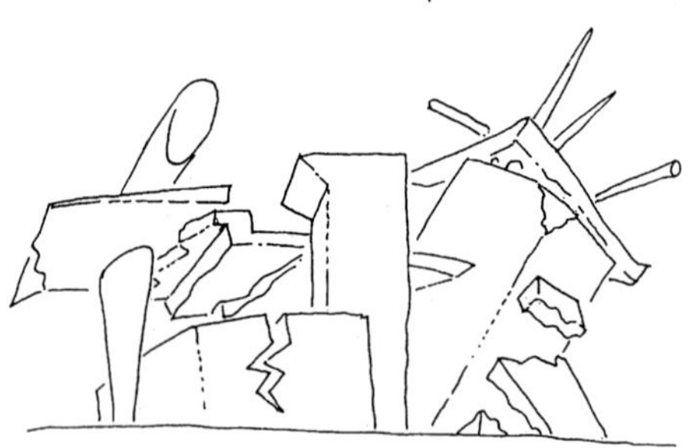

Award-winning Villa
after
Earthquake

LK 89

CUTTING HEDGE DESIGN

the new horizon——.COM

"THE AGGRESSSOR"

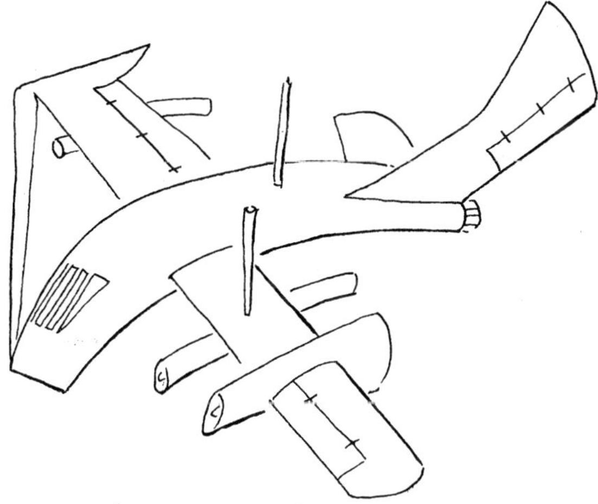

"THE NEW DISCORDE"

LK 90

Why should cars and planes forever remain classical, symetrical etc.......?

unsere Bürolandschaft

WHAT IF Nº 10 DOWNING STREET HAD NOT BEEN REBUILT BY RAYMOND ERITH ? LK 85

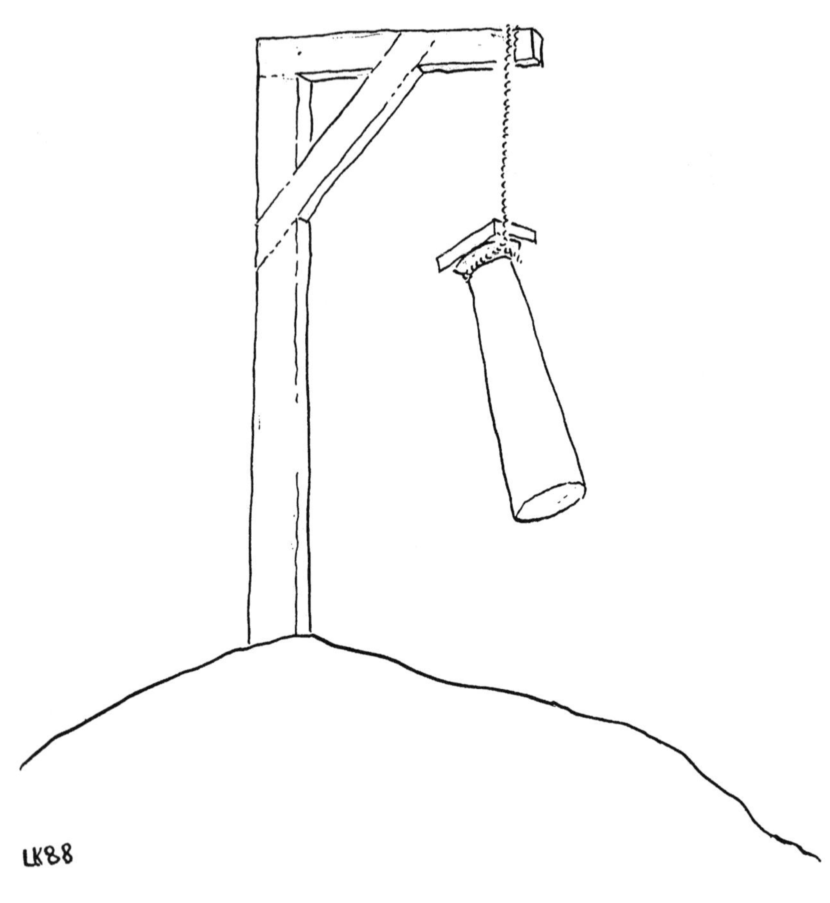

The Nüremberg-Tribunal of Architecture

москва
(1933)

Totalitarian
male & female
sex ~ symbols

Berlin
(1939)

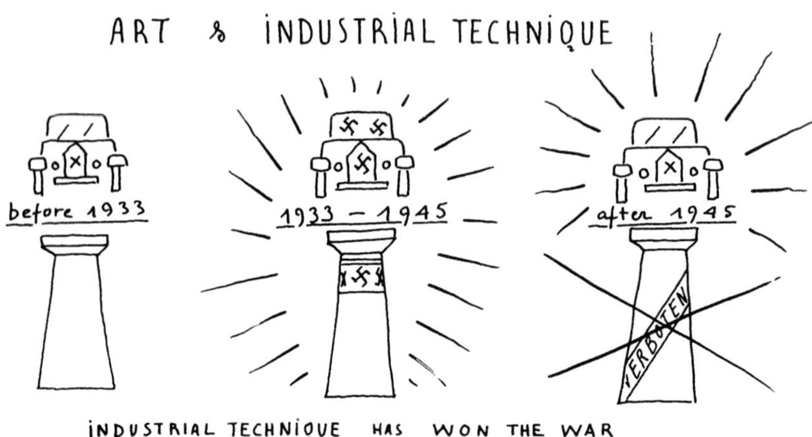

INDUSTRIAL TECHNIQUE HAS WON THE WAR
BECAUSE ART IS A DECEITFUL
WEAPON

LK81

oh GERMANY * BEWARE OF ART AND COLUMN

because only "TECHNOLOGY" will render invincible

* and others

Speer à Rio

Speer à Berlin

Speer à New York

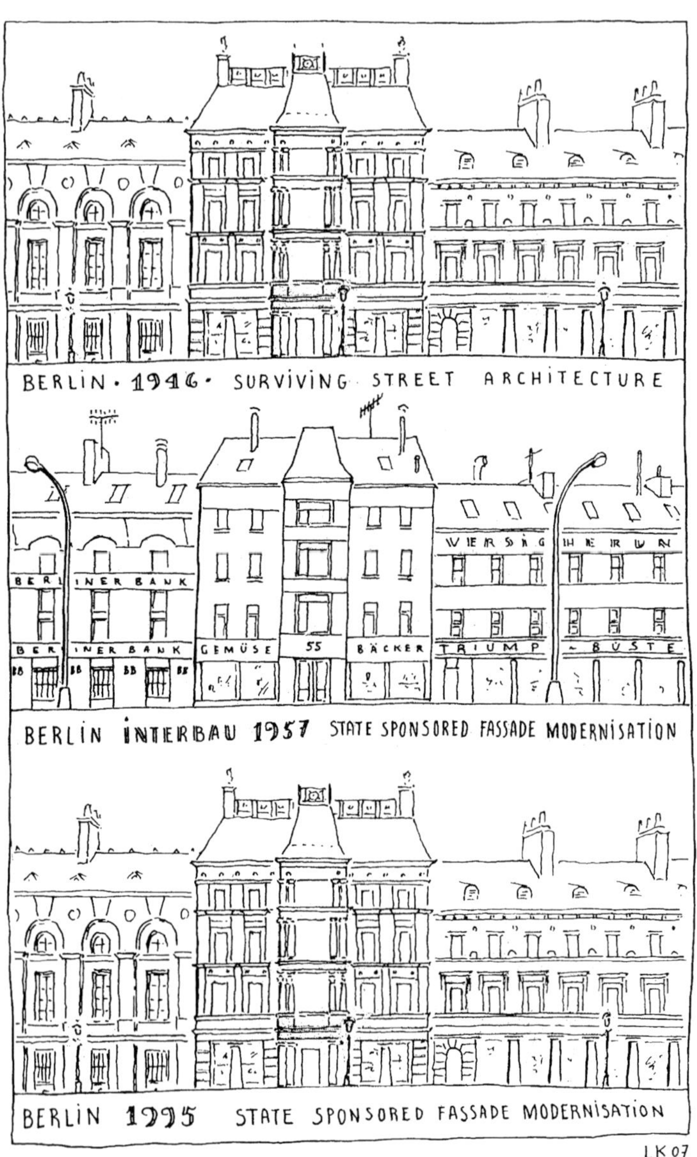
BERLIN · 1946 · SURVIVING STREET ARCHITECTURE
BER INER BANK
BER INER BANK
BB BB BB BB
GEMÜSE
55
BÄCKER
TRIUMP
BÜSTE
BERLIN INTERBAU 1957 STATE SPONSORED FASSADE MODERNISATION
BERLIN 1995 STATE SPONSORED FASSADE MODERNISATION
LK 07

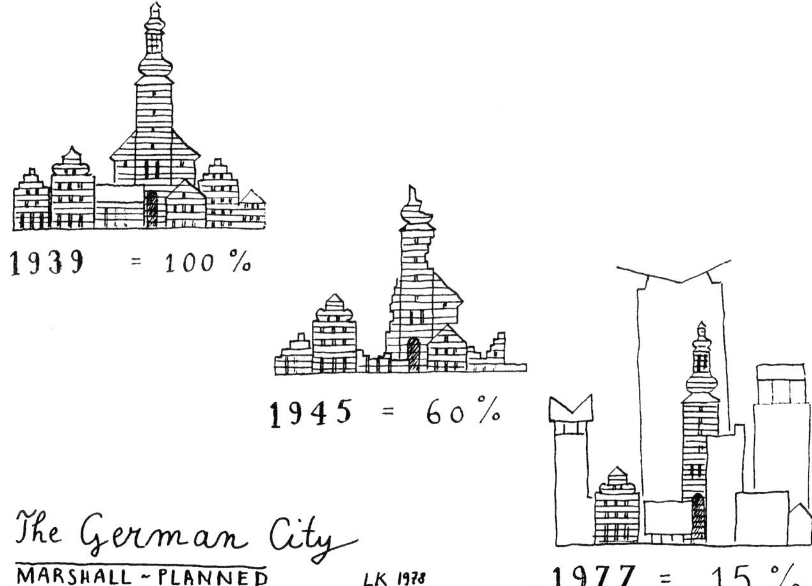
1939 = 100 %
1945 = 60 %
1977 = 15 %
The German City
MARSHALL - PLANNED
LK 1978

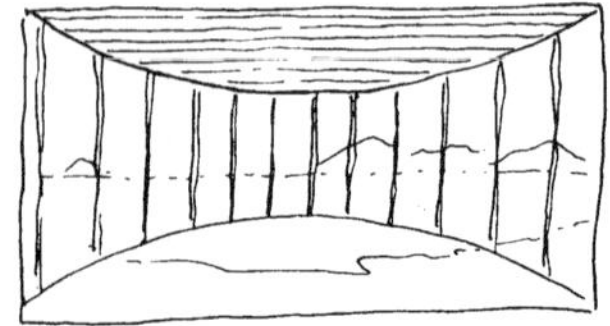
WORLD VIEWS
MODERNIST

CLASSICAL
LK
91

THE HIDDEN COROLLARY
of mental empires

"I am my only source of inspiration"..."I am only influenced by myself"..."God has sent me to"... "I am unlike any other"..."I am not influenced by anyone, only by events"..."I am the first!"..."I am your salv ... I am "The

"Those who are not for me are against me".
"I am the beginning and the End of... Philosophy science, architecture, mathematics, cooking, grammar, ..."
LK 06

la culture modern(ist)e

« MARQUE DEPOSÉE »

depuis 1920

LE COURAGE

LA NOSTALGIE

LK 99

THE SILLY "FLAT ROOF" FICTION

Practically speaking the flat roof is an impossibility

ITS FLAT!
ITS MODERN!

Logically speaking the flat roof is a paradox

a flat roof is no flatter than the earth is flat.....

the "flat roof" is a contradiction in terms

WATER HAS TO FLOW OFF SOMEWHERE,
to the OUTSIDE or the INSIDE.

LK05

The flat roof is no more 'modern' than the inclined roof is 'ancient'
The terraced or the pitched roofs are
TECHNOLOGICAL not EMOTIONAL or PHILOSOPHIC issues

YOU, SIR, ARE EXCEEDING THE INCLINE~LIMIT...
...IN THE NAME OF THE LAW, I MUST.... HM.........
SEVERELY FINE YOU.......HM...
BUT...
J THOUGHT
...?
WOUAH
15°
MAX. 8°
LK 07
STATUTORY HANDICAP RAMP
RESE

A SUFFERING MINORITY GROUP VENTING A LONG STANDING GRIEVANCE IN ORDERLY MANNER

WORLDCEILINGSCAPE

CULTURE-SCAPE

PRIVAT-SCAPE

CHURCH-SCAPE

OFFICE-SCAPE

FACTORYSCAPE

Dedicated to JAMES HILLMAN ~ LK 06

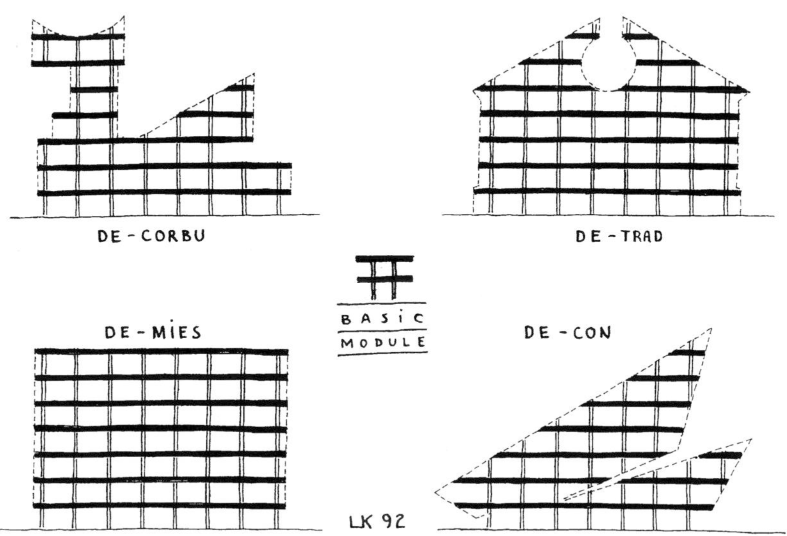

The Unified Field of New·Regional · Critical · Post · Structural·Anti·Classical
POST & NEO ~ MODERNISM
(before installation of CURTAIN WALL)

Choose from any
3 for 2
at Waterstone's